# Banking Services and its Operations

Dr.B. Thulasipriya

Published by

**BONFRING**®
Intellectual Integrity

**Banking Services and its Operations**



ISBN 978-93-85477-13-3

**Author**

Dr.B. Thulasipriya

**Bonfring**
309, 2nd Floor, 5th Street Extension, Gandhipuram,
Coimbatore-641 012.
Tamilnadu, India.
E-mail: info@bonfring.org
Website: www.bonfring.org
Phone: 0422-3928700

# Preface

Banking constitutes an important service. The banking sector acts as a strong pillar in financial system of our country. The recent developments in banking services and operators have a profound effect on the economic growth of our country.

Currently, the teaching practice of Banking operations and the financial services is more challenging due to contemporary developments in the worldwide financial system. Again there are lot of changes and updations in financial system which has a great impact on the development of the country.  Further, Banking has extended its services in the areas of financial markets to make system feasible.

This book is written for undergraduate students who are specialized in Banking & Financial Services. The topics are designed in accordance with Banking sector, financial system, its services and operations.

# Author Profile

**Dr.B. Thulasipriya**

Assistant Professor

Department of Commerce

PSGR Krishnammal College for Women

Coimbatore

**Dr.B. Thulasipriya,** M.Com., M.Phil., PGDCA., MBA., Ph.D., the author of this book titled **"Banking Services and its Operations"** has 12 years of teaching experience and about 9 years of Corporate Experience in the field of Company Audit. At present the author is working as an Assistant Professor belonging to the Department of Commerce with e-Commerce at PSGR Krishnammal College for Women, Coimbatore. The author has completed her UG and PG degree in Commerce at Avinashilingam Deemed University, Coimbatore and Annamalai University, Chidambaram. Further, she completed her M.Phil in Commerce in Bharathiar University, Coimbatore and further, she completed her PDGCA and MBA in Finance in Bharathiar University, Coimbatore. The author has participated, presented and published her research papers in National and International Conferences and in commerce and Management related journals.

| S.No | Contents | Page No |
|:---:|:---:|:---:|

| | | |
|---|---|---|
| **1** | **Banking: An Overview** | **1** |
| | Introduction | 1 |
| | Banking: Meaning | 1 |
| | Banking in India | 1 |
| | Banking Law | 2 |
| | Definition of a Bank | 3 |
| | Classification of Banks | 3 |
| **2** | **Commercial Banking** | **7** |
| | Meaning | 7 |
| | Definition | 7 |
| | Types of Banks | 7 |
| | Functions | 9 |
| **3** | **Financial System** | **16** |
| | Structure and Functions | 16 |
| | Classification of Financial Markets | 16 |
| | Capital Market | 18 |
| | Money Market | 19 |
| | Meaning of Money Market | 19 |
| | Role of Money Market in Economy | 20 |
| | Players of Money Market | 20 |
| | Functions of Money Markets | 20 |
| | Features of Money Market | 20 |
| | Functions of a Developed Money Market | 21 |
| | Components, Sub Markets of Indian Money Market | 22 |
| | Monetary Policy of India | 23 |
| | Objectives of Monetary Policy of India | 24 |
| | Monetary Policy of RBI | 25 |
| **4** | **Credit Control** | **27** |
| | Need for Credit Control | 27 |
| | Objectives of Credit Control | 27 |
| | Methods of Credit Control | 27 |
| | Qualitative Method | 27 |

| | | |
|---|---|---:|
| **5** | **Central Bank** | **29** |
| | Introduction | 29 |
| | Meaning | 29 |
| | Functions | 29 |
| **6** | **Banking Systems** | **32** |
| | Introduction to Banking Systems | 32 |
| | Role of Banking in India's Developing Economy | 33 |
| **7** | **State Bank of India** | **34** |
| | Introduction | 34 |
| | History | 34 |
| | Functions | 34 |
| | Associate Banks of SBI | 36 |
| **8** | **Co-operative Banks** | **37** |
| | Introduction | 37 |
| | History of Co-operative Banking in India | 38 |
| | Features of Co-operative Bank | 38 |
| | Structure of Co-operative Banking in India | 39 |
| | Urban Co-operative Banks | 39 |
| | Rural Co-Operatives | 39 |
| | Types of Co-operative Banks in India | 40 |
| | Functions of Co-Operative Banks | 41 |
| | Differences between Co-Operative Banks and Commercial Banks in India | 41 |
| **9** | **National Bank for Agriculture and Rural Development (NABARD)** | **43** |
| | Introduction | 43 |
| | Objectives | 43 |
| | Role of NABARD | 44 |
| | Functions of NABARD | 44 |
| **10** | **Globalisation of Banking** | **46** |
| | Technological Development | 46 |
| | Online Banking | 46 |
| | Automatic Teller Machine | 46 |
| | Tele Banking | 47 |

Electronic Clearing Service (ECS)     47

Electronic Funds Transfer (EFT)     47

Real Time Gross Settlement     47

Point of Sale Terminal     48

Satellite Banking     48

Phone Banking     48

BANCASSURANCE     49

Core Banking Solutions     50

Financial Electronic Data Interchange     51

International Banking     51

Risk Management     52

CRMS and ANY Branch Banking     52

INFINET     52

SWIFT     53

Universal Banking     53

Corporate Banking     55

**11    Credit Card     58**

Introduction     58

Anatomy of a Credit Card     58

Materials     60

Quality Control     60

Future Outlook     60

Operations of Credit Cards     60

Definitions     61

Types of Credit Cards     62

Comparison between Credit Card and Debit Card     67

Credit Card Operation     68

Parties Involved in a Credit Card     68

Calculation of Finance Charge     69

Advantages of Using a Credit Card     69

Disadvantages of Credit Cards     70

**12    Originations**                                                      **71**

Origination-Meaning                                                          71

Origination Elements                                                         71

Loan Processing                                                              72

Underwriting                                                                 72

Servicing                                                                    72

Loan Processing                                                              72

Traditional Steps                                                            73

Differences between an Underwriter and a Processor                          75

Strategic Importance of Credit Card Payments                                76

What to Look for in a Provider                                               76

Credit Card Reconciliation                                                   77

Purchasing Card Policy and Procedures                                       78

Cardholder Dispute                                                           80

**13    Mortgage**                                                          **81**

Introduction                                                                81

Basic Concepts and Legal Regulation                                         82

Loan and Mortgage Terminology                                               82

Types of Mortgage Loans                                                      84

Mortgage Underwriting                                                        84

Repaying the Mortgage                                                        86

Interest-only Lifetime Mortgage                                             87

Types of Reverse Mortgage Products                                          87

Pricing of Reverse Mortgage Products                                        88

Significance of Reverse Mortgage System in India                           88

Risk Inherent in the Reverse Mortgage Product                              88

Risk Mitigation                                                             89

Mortgage Originator                                                         89

Third-Party Mortgage Originator-Definition                                 89

Settlement Service: Meaning                                                 90

Underwriting                                                                91

3 C'S of Underwriting                                                       91

Types of Underwriting                                                       92

Importance of Underwriting                                                  92

| | | |
|---|---|---|
| **14** | **Indian Trade Market** | **94** |
| | Introduction to Indian Trade Market | 94 |
| | Trading | 94 |
| **15** | **Letter of Credit** | **96** |
| | Elements of a Letter of Credit | 96 |
| | Parties to Letter of Credit | 96 |
| | Documentation Requirements | 97 |
| | Characteristics of Letter of Credit | 98 |
| | Types and Features of Letters of Credit | 99 |
| | Benefits of a Letter of Credit | 100 |
| | Risks in Letter of Credit Transactions | 101 |
| | Documentary Collections | 101 |
| | Advantages and Disadvantages of Documentary Collection | 102 |
| | Risks in Documentary Collections | 103 |
| **16** | **Bank Guarantee** | **104** |
| | Operation of Bank Guarantees | 104 |
| | Advantages of Bank Guarantee | 104 |
| | Types of Bank Guarantee | 104 |
| **17** | **Loan** | **106** |
| | Introduction | 106 |
| | Types of Loans | 106 |

# 1. Banking: An Overview

## Introduction

Finance is the life blood of trade, commerce and industry. Now-a-days, banking sector acts as the backbone of modern business. Development of any country mainly depends upon the banking system.

The term bank is either derived from Old Italian word banca or from a French word banque both mean a Bench or money exchange table. In olden days, European money lenders or money changers used to display (show) coins of different countries in big heaps (quantity) on benches or tables for the purpose of lending or exchanging.

Indian banking is the lifeline of the nation and its people. Banking has helped in developing the vital sectors of the economy and usher in a new dawn of progress on the Indian horizon. The sector has translated the hopes and aspirations of millions of people into reality. But to do so, it has had to control miles and miles of difficult terrain, suffer the indignities of foreign rule and the pangs of partition. Today, Indian banks can confidently compete with modern banks of the world.

Before the 20th century, usury, or lending money at a high rate of interest, was widely prevalent in rural India. Entry of Joint stock banks and development of Cooperative movement have taken over a good deal of business from the hands of the Indian money lender, who although still exist, have lost his menacing teeth.

In the Indian Banking System, Cooperative banks exist side by side with commercial banks and play a supplementary role in providing need-based finance, especially for agricultural and agriculture-based operations including farming, cattle, milk, hatchery, personal finance etc. along with some small industries and self-employment driven activities.

## Banking: Meaning

A **bank** is a financial institution licensed as a receiver that accepts deposits from the public and creates credit. Lending activities can be performed either directly or indirectly through capital markets. Due to their importance in the financial system and influence on national economies, banks are highly regulated in most countries. In most countries, banks are regulated by the national government or central bank.

The majority nations have institutionalized a system known as fractional reserve banking under which banks hold liquid assets equal to only a portion of their current liabilities. In addition to other regulations intended to ensure liquidity, banks are generally subject to minimum capital requirements based on an international set of capital standards, known as the Basel Accords.

In general terms, the business activity of accepting and safeguarding money owned by other individuals and entities, and then lending out this money in order to earn a profit.

## Banking in India

Banking in India in the modern sense originated during the last decades of the 18th century. Among the first banks were the Bank of Hindustan, which was established in 1770 and liquidated in 1829-32; and the General Bank of India, established in 1786 but failed in 1791. The largest bank, and the oldest still in existence, is the State Bank of India (S.B.I). It originated as the Bank of Calcutta in June 1806. In 1809, it was renamed as the Bank of Bengal. This was one of the three banks funded by a presidency Government, the other two were the Bank of Bombay and the Bank of Madras. The three banks were merged in 1921 to form the Imperial Bank of India, which upon India's independence, became the State Bank of India in 1955.

For many years the presidency banks had acted as quasi-central banks, as did their successors, until the Reserve Bank of India was established in 1935, under the Reserve Bank of India Act, 1934.

In 1960, the State Banks of India was given control of eight state-associated banks under the State Bank of India (Subsidiary Banks) Act, 1959. These are now called its associate banks. In 1969 the Indian government nationalised 14 major private banks. In 1980, 6 more private banks were nationalised. These nationalised banks are the majority of lenders in the Indian economy. They dominate the banking sector because of their large size and widespread networks.

The Indian banking sector is broadly classified into scheduled banks and non-scheduled banks. The scheduled banks are those which are included under the 2nd Schedule of the Reserve Bank of India Act, 1934. The scheduled banks are further classified into: nationalised banks; State Bank of India and its associates; Regional Rural Banks (RRBs); foreign banks; and other Indian private sector banks. The term commercial banks refer to both scheduled and non-scheduled commercial banks which are regulated under the Banking Regulation Act, 1949.

Generally banking in India is fairly mature in terms of supply, product range and reach even though reach in rural India and to the poor still remains a challenge. The Government has developed initiatives to address this through the State Bank of India expanding its branch network and through the National Bank for Agriculture and Rural Development with facilities like microfinance.

## Banking Law

Banking law is based on a contractual analysis of the relationship between the **bank** and **customer** defined as any entity for which the bank agrees to conduct an account.

The law implies rights and obligations into this relationship as follows:

- The bank account balance is the financial position between the bank and the customer: when the account is in credit, the bank owes the balance to the customer; when the account is overdrawn, the customer owes the balance to the bank.
- The bank agrees to pay the customer's cheques up to the amount standing to the credit of the customer's account, plus any agreed overdraft limit.
- The bank may not pay from the customer's account without a mandate from the customer, e.g. cheques drawn by the customer.
- The bank agrees to promptly collect the cheques deposited to the customer's account as the customer's agent, and to credit the proceeds to the customer's account.
- The bank has a right to combine the customer's accounts, since each account is just an aspect of the same credit relationship.
- The bank has a lien on cheques deposited to the customer's account, to the extent that the customer is indebted to the bank.
- The bank must not disclose details of transactions through the customer's account unless the customer consents, there is a public duty to disclose, the bank's interests require it, or the law demands it.
- The bank must not close a customer's account without reasonable notice, since cheques are outstanding in the ordinary course of business for several days.

These implied contractual terms may be modified by express agreement between the customer and the bank. The statutes and regulations in force within a particular jurisdiction may also modify the above terms or create new rights, obligations or limitations relevant to the bank-customer relationship.

## Definition of a Bank

*The term 'Bank' has been defined in different ways by different economists. A few definitions are:*

According to Walter Leaf "A bank is a person or corporation which holds it out to receive from the public, deposits payable on demand by cheque."

Horace White has defined a bank, "as a manufacture of credit and a machine for facilitating exchange."

According to Prof. Kinley, "A bank is an establishment which makes to individuals such advances of money as may be required and safely made, and to which individuals entrust money when not required by them for use.

The Banking Companies Act of India defines Bank as "A Bank is a financial institution which accepts money from the public for the purpose of lending or investment repayable on demand or otherwise withdrawable by cheques, drafts or order or otherwise."

Thus, a bank is a financial institution which deals in debts and credits. It accepts deposits, lends money and also creates money. It bridges the gap between the savers and borrowers. Banks are not merely traders in money but also manufacturers of money.

In simple words, Banking can be defined as the business activity of accepting and safeguarding money owned by other individuals and entities, and then lending out this money in order to earn a profit.   However, with the means of access of time, the activities covered by banking business have widened and now various other services are also offered by banks.  The banking services these days include issuance of debit and credit cards, providing safe custody of valuable items, lockers, ATM services and online transfer of funds globally.

## Classification of Banks

Indian banking industry has been divided into two parts, organized and unorganized sectors. The organized sector consists of Reserve Bank of India, Commercial Banks and Co-operative Banks, and Specialized Financial Institutions (IDBI, ICICI, IFC etc). The unorganized sector, which is not homogeneous, is largely made up of money lenders and indigenous bankers.

An outline of the Indian Banking structure may be presented as follows:

1. Reserve banks of India.
2. Indian Scheduled Commercial Banks.
   a. State Bank of India and its associate banks.
   b. Twenty nationalized banks.
   c. Regional rural banks.
   d. Other scheduled commercial banks.
3. Foreign Banks.
4. Non-scheduled Banks.
5. Co-operative Banks.

## a.  Central Bank

A bank which is entrusted with the functions of guiding and regulating the banking system of a country is known as its Central bank. Such a bank does not deal with the general public. It acts essentially as Government's banker, as to maintain deposit accounts of all other banks and advances money to other banks, when needed. The Central Bank provides guidance to other banks whenever they face any problem. It is therefore known as the banker's bank. The Reserve Bank of India is the central bank of our country.

The Central Bank maintains record of Government revenue and expenditure under various heads. It also advises the Government on monetary and credit policies and decides on the interest rates for bank deposits and bank loans. In addition, foreign exchange rates are also determined by the central bank. Another important function of the Central Bank is the issuance of currency notes, regulating their circulation in the country by different methods. No other bank than the Central Bank can issue currency.

## b.  Commercial Banks

Commercial Banks are banking institutions that accept deposits and grant short-term loans and advances to their customers. In addition to giving short-term loans, commercial banks also give medium-term and long-term loan to business enterprises. Now-a-days some of the commercial banks are also providing housing loan on a long-term basis to individuals. There are also many other functions of commercial banks, which are discussed later in this lesson.

*Types of Commercial Banks*

Commercial banks are of three types i.e., Public sector banks, Private sector banks and foreign banks.

i.  **Public Sector Banks**: These are banks where majority stake is held by the Government of India or Reserve Bank of India. Examples of public sector banks are: State Bank of India, Corporation Bank, Bank of Baroda and Dena Bank, etc.

ii.  **Private Sectors Banks**: In case of private sector banks majority of share capital of the bank is held by private individuals. These banks are registered as companies with limited liability. For example: The Jammu and Kashmir Bank Ltd., Bank of Rajasthan Ltd., Development Credit Bank Ltd, Lord Krishna Bank Ltd., Bharat Overseas Bank Ltd., Global Trust Bank, Vysya Bank, etc.

iii.  **Foreign Banks**: These banks are registered and have their headquarters in a foreign country but operate their branches in our country. Some of the foreign banks operating in our country are Hong Kong and Shanghai Banking Corporation (HSBC), Citibank, American Express Bank, Standard & Chartered Bank, Grindlay's Bank, etc. The number of foreign banks operating in our country has increased since the financial sector reforms of 1991.

## c.  Development Banks

Business often requires medium and long-term capital for purchase of machinery and equipment, for using latest technology, or for expansion and modernization. Such financial assistance is provided by Development Banks. They also undertake other development measures like subscribing to the shares and debentures issued by companies, in case of under subscription of the issue by the public. Industrial Finance Corporation of India (IFCI) and State Financial Corporations (SFCs) are examples of development banks in India.

## d.  Co-operative Banks

People who come together to jointly serve their common interest often form a co-operative society under the Co-operative Societies Act. When a co-operative society engages itself in banking business it is called a Co-operative Bank. The society has to obtain a licence from the Reserve Bank of India before starting banking business. Any co-operative bank as a society is to function under the overall supervision of the Registrar, Co-operative Societies of the State. As regards banking business, the society must follow the guidelines set and issued by the Reserve Bank of India.

*Types of Co-operative Banks*

There are three types of co-operative banks operating in our country. They are primary credit societies, central co-operative banks and state co-operative banks. These banks are organized at three levels, village or town level, district level and state level.

i. **Primary Credit Societies**: These are formed at the village or town level with borrower and non-borrower members residing in one locality. The operations of each society are restricted to a small area so that the members know each other and are able to watch over the activities of all members to prevent frauds.

ii. **Central Co-operative Banks**: These banks operate at the district level having some of the primary credit societies belonging to the same district as their members. These banks provide loans to their members (i.e., primary credit societies) and function as a link between the primary credit societies and state co-operative banks.

iii. **State Co-operative Banks**: These are the apex (highest level) co-operative banks in all the states of the country. They mobilise funds and help in its proper channelisation among various sectors. The money reaches the individual borrowers from the state co-operative banks through the central co-operative banks and the primary credit societies.

## e. Specialised Banks

There are some banks, which cater to the requirements and provide overall support for setting up business in specific areas of activity. EXIM Bank, SIDBI and NABARD are examples of such banks. They engage themselves in some specific area or activity and thus, are called specialised banks.

i. **Export Import Bank of India (EXIM Bank)**: If needed to set up a business for exporting products abroad or importing products from foreign countries for sale in our country, EXIM bank can provide the required support and assistance. The bank grants loans to exporters and importers and also provides information about the international market. It gives guidance about the opportunities for export or import, the risks involved in it and the competition to be faced, etc.

ii. **Small Industries Development Bank of India (SIDBI):** If needed to establish a small-scale business unit or industry, loan on easy terms can be available through SIDBI. It also finances modernisation of small-scale industrial units, use of new technology and market activities. The aim and focus of SIDBI is to promote, finance and develop small-scale industries.

iii. **National Bank for Agricultural and Rural Development (NABARD):** It is a central or apex institution for financing agricultural and rural sectors. If a person is engaged in agriculture or other activities like handloom weaving, fishing, etc. NABARD can provide credit, both short-term and long-term, through regional rural banks. It provides financial assistance, especially, to co-operative credit, in the field of agriculture, small-scale industries, cottage and village industries handicrafts and allied economic activities in rural areas.

## Features of a Bank

### 1. *Dealing in Money*

Bank is a financial institution which deals with other people's money i.e. money given by depositors.

### 2. *Individual / Firm / Company*

A bank may be a person, firm or a company. A banking company means a company which is in the business of banking.

### 3. *Acceptance of Deposit*

A bank accepts money from the people in the form of deposits which are usually repayable on demand or after the expiry of a fixed period. It gives safety to the deposits of its customers. It also acts as a custodian of funds of its customers.

### 4. *Giving Advances*

A bank lends out money in the form of loans to those who require it for different purposes.

### 5. *Payment and Withdrawal*

A bank provides easy payment and withdrawal facility to its customers in the form of cheques and drafts, It also brings bank money in circulation. This money is in the form of cheques, drafts, etc.

### 6. *Agency and Utility Services*

A bank provides various banking facilities to its customers. They include general utility services and agency services.

### 7. *Profit and Service Orientation*

A bank is a profit seeking institution having service oriented approach.

### 8. *Ever Increasing Functions*

Banking is an evolutionary concept. There is continuous expansion and diversification as regards the functions, services and activities of a bank.

### 9. *Connecting Link*

A bank acts as a connecting link between borrowers and lenders of money. Banks collect money from those who have surplus money and give the same to those who are in need of money.

### 10. *Banking Business*

A bank's main activity should be to do business of banking which should not be subsidiary to any other business.

### 11. *Name Identity*

A bank should always add the word "bank" to its name to enable people to know that it is a bank and that it is dealing in money.

# 2. Commercial Banking

A commercial bank is a profit-seeking business firm, dealing in money and credit. It is a financial institution dealing in money in the sense that it accepts deposits of money from the public to keep them in its custody for safety. So also, it deals in credit, i.e., it creates credit by making advances out of the funds received as deposits to needy people. It thus, functions as a mobiliser of saving in the economy. A bank is, therefore like a reservoir into which flow the savings, the idle surplus money of households and from which loans are given on interest to businessmen and others who need them for investment or productive use.

## Meaning

A **commercial bank** is a financial institution that is authorized by law to receive money from businesses and individuals and lend money to them. Commercial banks are open to the public and serve individuals, institutions, and businesses. A commercial bank is almost certainly the type of bank because it is the type of bank that most people regularly use. Banks are regulated by federal and state laws depending on how they are organized and the services they provide. Commercial banks are also monitored through the Federal Reserve System.

## Definition

A **commercial bank** is a financial institution that is authorized by law to receive money from businesses and individuals and lend money to them. Commercial banks are open to the public and serve individuals, institutions, and businesses. Banks are regulated by federal and state laws depending on how they are organized and the services they provide. Commercial banks are also monitored through the Federal Reserve System.

## Types of Banks

Banks can be classified into commercial banks and central bank. Commercial banks are those which provide banking services for profit. The central bank has the function of controlling commercial banks and various other economic activities. There are many types of commercial banks such as deposit banks, industrial banks, savings banks, agricultural banks, exchange banks, and miscellaneous bank.

### 1. Deposit Banks

The most important type of deposit banks is the commercial banks. They have connection with the commercial class of people. These banks accept deposits from the public and lend them to needy parties. Since their deposits are for short period only, these banks extend loans only for a short period. Ordinarily these banks lend money for a period between 3 to 6 months. They do not like to lend money for long periods or to invest their funds in any way in long term securities.

### 2. Industrial Banks

Industries require a huge capital for a long period to buy machinery and equipment. Industrial banks help such industrialists. They provide long term loans to industries. Besides, they buy shares and debentures of companies, and enable them to have fixed capital. Sometimes, they even underwrite the debentures and shares of big industrial concerns.

The important functions of industrial banks are:

- They accept long term deposits.
- They meet the credit requirements of industries by extending long term loans.
- These banks advise the industrial firms regarding the sale and purchase of shares and debentures.

The industrial banks play a vital role in accelerating industrial development. In India, after attainment of independence, several industrial banks were started with large paid up capital. They are, The Industrial Finance Corporation (I.F.C.), The State Financial Corporations (S.F.C.), Industrial Credit and Investment Corporation of India (ICICI) and Industrial Development Bank of India (IDBI) etc.

### 3. Savings Banks

These banks were specially established to encourage thrift among small savers and therefore, they were willing to accept small sums as deposits. They encourage savings of the poor and middle class people. In India we do not have such special institutions, but post offices perform such functions. After nationalisation most of the nationalised banks accept the saving deposits.

### 4. Agricultural Banks

Agriculture has its own problems and hence there are separate banks to finance it. These banks are organised on co-operative lines and therefore do not work on the principle of maximum profit for the shareholders. These banks meet the credit requirements of the farmers through term loans, viz., short, medium and long term loans.

There are two types of agricultural banks:

a) Agricultural Co-operative Banks, and
b) Land Mortgage Banks.

Co-operative Banks are mainly for short periods. For long periods there are Land Mortgage Banks. Both these types of banks are performing useful functions in India.

### 5. Exchange Banks

These banks finance mostly for the foreign trade of a country. Their main function is to discount, accept and collect foreign bills of exchange. They buy and sell foreign currency and thus help businessmen in their transactions. They also carry on the ordinary banking business.

In India, there are some commercial banks which are branches of foreign banks. These banks facilitate for the conversion of Indian currency into foreign currency to make payments to foreign exporters. They purchase bills from exporters and sell their proceeds to importers. They purchase and sell "forward exchange" too and thus minimise the difference in exchange rates between different periods, and also protect merchants from losses arising out of exchange fluctuations by bearing the risk. The industrial and commercial development of a country depends these days, largely upon the efficiency of these institutions.

### 6. Miscellaneous Banks

There are certain kinds of banks which have arisen in due course to meet the specialised needs of the people. In England and America, there are investment banks whose object is to control the distribution of capital into several uses.

American Trade Unions have got labour banks, where the savings of the labourers are pooled together. In London, there is the London Discount House whose business is "to go about the city seeking for bills to discount." There are numerous types of different banks in the world, carrying on one or the other banking business.

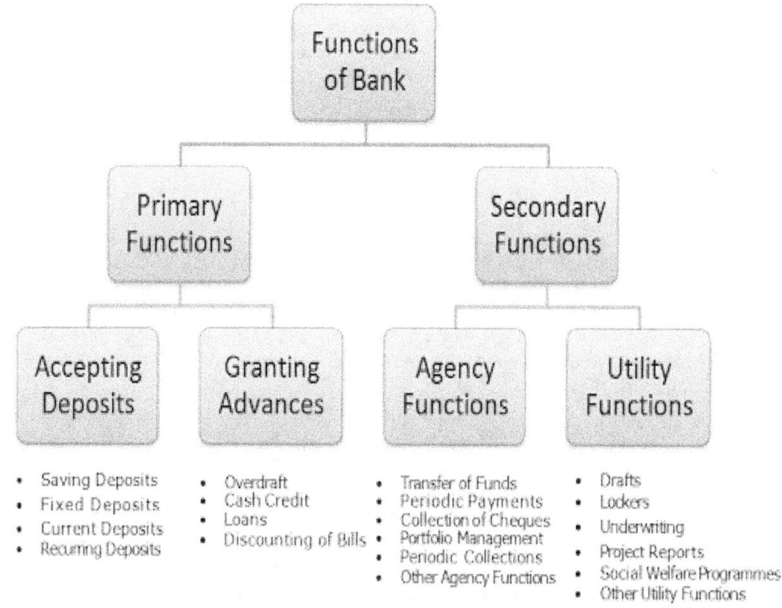


## Functions

Commercial banks have to perform a variety of functions which are common to both developed and developing countries. These are known as 'General Banking' functions of the commercial banks. The modern banks perform a variety of functions.

These can be broadly divided into two categories:

a) Primary functions and
b) Secondary function

## A. Primary Functions

Primary banking functions of the commercial banks include:

1. Acceptance of deposits
2. Advancing loans
3. Creation of credit
4. Clearing of cheques
5. Financing foreign trade
6. Remittance of funds

## 1. Accepting Deposits

The most important function of commercial banks is to accept deposits from the public. Various sections of society, according to their needs and economic condition, deposit their savings with the banks. Accepting deposits is the primary function of a commercial bank mobilise savings of the household sector.

For example, fixed and low income group people deposit their savings in small amounts from the points of view of security, income and saving promotion. On the other hand, traders and businessmen deposit their savings in the banks for the convenience of payment. Therefore, keeping the needs and interests of various sections of society, banks formulate various deposit schemes. Banks generally accept three types of deposits viz.,

    a)   Current Deposits
    b)   Savings Deposits, and
    c)   Fixed Deposits.

### a. Current Deposits

The depositors of such deposits can withdraw and deposit money whenever they desire at any time. Since banks have to keep the deposited amount of such accounts in cash always, they carry either no interest or very low rate of interest. The customer is required to leave a minimum balance undrawn with the bank. Cheques are used to withdraw the amount. These deposits are called as Demand Deposits because these can be demanded or withdrawn by the depositors at any time they want.

Such deposit accounts are highly useful for traders, industrialists and big business firms who receive and make Commercial Banking large payments because they have to make payments and accept payments many times in a day. The bank levies certain incidental charges on the customer for the services rendered by it.

### b. Fixed Deposits

These are the deposits which are deposited for a definite period of time. This period is generally not less than one year and, therefore, these are called as long term deposits. These deposits cannot be withdrawn before the expiry of the stipulated time for which they are deposited or without giving a prior notice for withdrawal and, therefore, these are also called as time deposits.

If the depositor is in need of money, he has to borrow on the security of this account and pay a slightly higher rate of interest to the bank. They are attracted by the payment of interest which is usually higher for longer period. Fixed deposits are liked by depositors both for their safety and as well as for their interest.

In India, they are accepted between three months and ten years. These deposits generally carry a higher rate of interest because banks can use these deposits for a definite time without having the fear of being withdrawn.

### c. Saving Deposits

This is meant mainly for professional men and middle class people to help them deposit their small savings. It can be opened without any introduction. Money can be deposited at any time but the maximum cannot go beyond a certain limit. There is a restriction on the amount that can be deposited and withdrawn at a particular time up to a certain limit once or twice in a week. If the customer wishes to withdraw more than the specified amount at any one time, he has to give prior notice. Interest is allowed on the credit balance of this account. The rate of interest is very less. As is evident from the name of such deposits their main objective is to mobilise small savings in the form of deposits. These deposits are generally done by salaried people and the people who have fixed and less income. This system greatly encourages the habit of thrift or savings.

## 2. Advancing Loans

The second primary function of a commercial bank is to make loans and advances to all types of persons, particularly to businessmen and entrepreneurs. Banks charge interest from the borrowers and this is the main source of their income. Banks advance loans not only on the basis of the deposits of the public rather they also advance loans on the basis of depositing the money in the accounts of borrowers.

Loans are made against personal security, out of deposits, gold and silver, stocks of goods and other assets. In other words, at the time of advancing loans, they demand proper security or collateral. This is called as credit creation by commercial banks.

Modern banks give mostly secured loans for productive purposes. Generally, the value of security or collateral is equal to the amount of loan. This is done mainly with a view to recover the loan money by selling the security in the event of non-refund of the loan. At limes, banks give loan on the basis of personal security also. Therefore, such loans are called as unsecured loan. Banks generally give following types of loans and advances:

### a. Cash Credit

In this type of credit scheme, banks advance loans to its customers on the basis of bonds, inventories and other approved securities. But the entire loan is not given at one particular time, instead the amount is credited into his account in the bank and cash will be given in intervals. Under this scheme, banks enter into an agreement with its customers to which money can be withdrawn many times with a small sums of money according to his requirements through cheques, but he cannot exceed the credit limit allowed to him. The customer is required to pay interest only on the amount of credit availed to him. Under this set up banks open accounts of their customers and deposit the loan money. With this type of loan, credit is created. Besides, the bank can also give specified loan to a person, for a firm against some collateral security. The bank can recall such loans at its option.

### b. Money at Call

Bank also grant loans for a very short period, generally not exceeding 7 days to the borrowers, usually dealers or brokers in stock exchange markets against collateral securities like stock or equity shares, debentures, etc., offered by them. Such advances are repayable immediately at short notice hence; they are described as money at call or call money.

### c. Demand Loans

These are such loans that can be recalled on demand by the banks. The entire loan amount is paid in lump sum by crediting it to the loan account of the borrower, and thus entire loan becomes chargeable to interest with immediate effect.

### d. Short-term Loan

These loans may be given as personal loans, loans to finance working capital or as priority sector advances. These are made against some security and entire loan amount is transferred to the loan account of the borrower.

### e. Term Loans

Banks give term loans to traders, industrialists and now to agriculturists also against some collateral securities. Term loans are so-called because their maturity period varies between 1 to 10 years. Term loans, as such provide intermediate or working capital funds to the borrowers. Sometimes, two or more banks may jointly provide large term loans to the borrower against a common security. Such loans are called participation loans or consortium finance.

*f. Consumer Credit*

Banks also grant credit to households in a limited amount to buy some durable consumer goods such as television sets, refrigerators, etc., or to meet some personal needs like payment of hospital bills etc. Such consumer credit is made in a lump sum and is repayable in installments in a short time. Under the 20-point programme, the scope of consumer credit has been extended to cover expenses on marriage, funeral etc., as well.

## 3. Over-Draft

In this case, the depositor in a current account is allowed to draw over and above his account up to a previously agreed limit. Banks advance loans to its customer's upto a certain amount through over-drafts, if there are no deposits in the current account. For this banks demand a security from the customers and charge very high rate of interest. The bank, however, charges interest only on the amount overdrawn from the account. This type of loan is very popular with the Indian businessmen.

## 4. Discounting of Bills of Exchange

This is the most prevalent and important method of advancing loans to the traders for short-term purposes. This is another type of lending which is very popular with the modern banks. Under this system, banks advance loans to the traders and business firms by discounting their bills. The holder of a bill can get it discounted by the bank, when he is in need of money. After deducting its commission, the bank Banking pays the present price of the bill to the holder. Such bills form good investment for a bank. In this way, businessmen get loans on the basis of their bills of exchange before the time of their maturity. The commercial banks can rediscount, the discounted bills with the central banks when they are in need of money. These bills are safe and secured bills. When the bill matures the bank can secure its payment from the party which had accepted the bill.

## 5. Investment of Funds

The banks invest their surplus funds in three types of securities like Government securities, other approved securities and other securities. Government securities include both, central and state governments, such as treasury bills, national savings certificate etc.

Other securities include securities of state associated bodies like electricity boards, housing boards, debentures of Land Development Banks units of UTI, shares of Regional Rural banks etc.

## 6. Creation of Credit

A unique function of the bank is to create credit. Banks supply money to traders and manufacturers. They also create or manufacture money. Bank deposits are regarded as money. They are as good as cash. The reason is they can be used for the purchase of goods and services and also in payment of debts. When a bank grants a loan to its customer, it does not pay cash. It simply credits the account of the borrower. He can withdraw the amount whenever he wants by a cheque. In this case, bank has created a deposit without receiving cash. That is, banks are said to have created credit. Sayers says "banks are not merely purveyors of money, but also in an important sense, manufacturers of money."

## 7. Promote the Use of Cheques

The commercial banks render an important service by providing to their customers a cheap medium of exchange like cheques. It is found much more convenient to settle debts through cheques rather than through the use of cash. The cheque is the most developed type of credit instrument in the money market.

## 8. Agency Functions

Banks function in the form of agents and representatives of their customers. Customers give their consent for performing such functions. The important functions of these types are as follows:

i. Banks collect cheques, drafts, bills of exchange and dividends of the shares for their customers.
ii. Banks make payment for their clients and at times accept the bills of exchange: of their customers for which payment is made at the fixed time.
iii. Banks pay insurance premium of their customers. Besides this, they also deposit loan installments, income-tax, interest etc. as per directions.
iv. Banks purchase and sell securities, shares and debentures on behalf of their customers.
v. Banks arrange to send money from one place to another for the convenience of their customers.

## 9. Miscellaneous Functions

Besides the functions mentioned above, banks perform many other functions of general utility which are as follows:

i. Banks make arrangement of lockers for the safe custody of valuable assets of their customers such as gold, silver, legal documents etc.
ii. Banks give reference for their customers.
iii. Banks collect necessary and useful statistics relating to trade and industry.
iv. For facilitating foreign trade, banks undertake to sell and purchase foreign exchange.
v. Banks advise their clients relating to investment decisions as specialist
vi. Bank does the under-writing of shares and debentures also.
vii. Banks issue letters of credit.
viii. During natural calamities, banks are highly useful in mobilizing funds and donations.
ix. Banks provide loans for consumer durables like Car, Air-conditioner, and Fridge etc.

## 10. Miscellaneous Advances

Among other forms of bank advances there are packing credits given to exporters for a short duration, export bills purchased/discounted, import finance-advances against import bills, finance to the self employed, credit to the public sector, credit to the cooperative sector and above all, credit to the weaker sections of the community at concessional rates.

## 11. Financing Internal and Foreign Trade

The bank finances internal and foreign trade through discounting of exchange bills. Sometimes, the bank gives short-term loans to traders on the security of commercial papers. This discounting business greatly facilitates the movement of internal and external trade.

## 12. Remittance of Funds

Commercial banks, on account of their network of branches throughout the country, also provide facilities to remit funds from one place to another for their customers by issuing bank drafts, mail transfers or telegraphic transfers on nominal commission charges. As compared to the postal money orders or other instruments, bank drafts have proved to be a much cheaper mode of transferring money and have helped the business community considerably.

## B.  Secondary Functions

Secondary banking functions of the commercial banks include:

1.   Agency Services
2.   General Utility Services

These are discussed below.

## 1.  Agency Services

Banks also perform certain agency functions for and on behalf of their customers. The agency services are of immense value to the people at large.

The various agency services rendered by banks are as follows:

### a.  Collection and Payment of Credit Instruments

Banks collect and pay various credit instruments like cheques, bills of exchange, promissory notes etc., on behalf of their customers.

### b.  Purchase and Sale of Securities

Banks purchase and sell various securities like shares, stocks, bonds, debentures on behalf of their customers.

### c.  Collection of Dividends on Shares

Banks collect dividends and interest on shares and debentures of their customers and credit them to their accounts.

### d.  Acts as Correspondent

Sometimes banks act as representative and correspondents of their customers. They get passports, traveller's tickets and even secure air and sea passages for their customers.

### e.  Income-tax Consultancy

Banks may also employ income tax experts to prepare income tax returns for their customers and to help them to get refund of income tax.

### f.  Execution of Standing Orders

Banks execute the standing instructions of their customers for making various periodic payments. They pay subscriptions, rents, insurance premia etc., on behalf of their customers.

### g.  Acts as Trustee and Executor

Banks preserve the 'Wills' of their customers and execute them after their death.

## 2.  General Utility Services

In addition to agency services, the modern banks provide many general utility services for the community as given.

### a.  Locker Facility

Bank provides locker facility to their customers. The customers can keep their valuables, such as gold and silver ornaments, important documents; shares and debentures in these lockers for safe custody.

### b.  Traveller's Cheques and Credit Cards

Banks issue traveller's  cheques to help their customers to travel without the fear of theft or loss of money. With this facility, the customers need not take the risk of carrying cash with them during their travels.

*c. Letter of Credit*

Letters of credit are issued by the banks to their customers certifying their credit worthiness. Letters of credit are very useful in foreign trade.

*d. Collection of Statistics*

Banks collect statistics giving important information relating to trade, commerce, industries, money and banking. They also publish valuable journals and bulletins containing articles on economic and financial matters.

*e. Acting Referee*

Banks may act as referees with respect to the financial standing, business reputation and respectability of customers.

*f. Underwriting Securities*

Banks underwrite the shares and debentures issued by the Government, public or private companies.

*g. Gift Cheques*

Some banks issue cheques of various denominations to be used on auspicious occasions.

*h. Accepting Bills of Exchange on Behalf of Customers*

Sometimes, banks accept bills of exchange, internal as well as foreign, on behalf of their customers. It enables customers to import goods.

*i. Merchant Banking*

Some commercial banks have opened merchant banking divisions to provide merchant banking services.

## C. Fulfillment of Socio-Economic Objectives

In recent years, commercial banks, particularly in developing countries, have been called upon to help achieve certain socio-economic objectives laid down by the state. For example, the nationalized banks in India have framed special innovative schemes of credit to help small agriculturists, village and cottage industries, retailers, artisans, the self employed persons through loans and advances at concessional rates of interest.

Under the Differential Interest Scheme (D.I.S.) the nationalized banks in India advance loans to persons belonging to scheduled tribes, tailors, rickshaw-walas, shoe-makers at the concessional rate of 4 per cent per annum. This does not cover even the cost of the funds made available to these priority sectors. Banking is, thus, being used to sub serve the national policy objectives of reducing inequalities of income and wealth, removal of poverty and elimination of unemployment in the country.

It is clear from the above that banks help development of trade and industry in the country. They encourage habits of thrift and saving. They help capital formation in the country. They lend money to traders and manufacturers. In the modern world, banks are to be considered not merely as dealers in money but also the leaders in economic development.

# 3. Financial System

## Structure and Functions

The **financial system** plays the key role in the economy by stimulating economic growth, influencing economic performance of the actors, affecting economic welfare. This is achieved by financial infrastructure, in which entities with funds allocate those funds to those who have potentially more productive ways to invest those funds. A financial system makes it possible a more efficient transfer of funds. As one party of the transaction may possess superior information than the other party, it can lead to the information asymmetry problem and inefficient allocation of financial resources. By overcoming the information asymmetry problem the financial system facilitates balance between those with funds to invest and those needing funds.

According to the **structural approach,** the financial system of an economy consists of three main components:

1. Financial markets.
2. Financial intermediaries (institutions).
3. Financial regulators.

Each of the components plays a specific role in the economy.

According to the functional approach, **financial markets** facilitate the flow of funds in order to finance investments by corporations, governments and individuals.

**Financial institutions** are the key players in the financial markets as they perform the function of intermediation and thus determine the flow of funds. The **financial regulators** perform the role of monitoring and regulating the participants in the financial system.

## Classification of Financial Markets

There different ways to classify financial markets. They are classified according to the financial instruments they are trading, features of services they provide, trading procedures, key market participants, as well as the origin of the markets.

From the perspective of country origin, its financial market can be broken down into an internal market and an external market.

The **Internal Market**, also called the **National Market**, consists of two parts:

a) Domestic market and
b) Foreign market.

The **Domestic Market** is where issuers domiciled in the country issue securities and where those securities are subsequently traded.

The **Foreign Market** is where securities are sold and traded outside the country of issuers.

The **External Market** also referred to as the **International Market, Offshore Market**, and the **Euro market** is the market where securities with the following two distinguishing features are trading:

a. At issuance they are offered simultaneously to investors in a number of countries; and
b. They are issued outside the jurisdiction of any single country.

*Classification on the Basis of Maturity of Claims*

On this basis, financial markets may be classified into money market and capital market.

**Money market:** A market where short term funds are borrowed and lend is called money market. **Money Market** is the sector of the financial market that includes financial instruments that have a maturity or redemption date that is one year or less at the time of issuance. These are mainly **Wholesale Markets**. Liquid funds as well as highly liquid securities are traded in the money market.

Examples of money market are Treasury bill market, call money market, commercial bill market etc. The main participants in this market are banks, financial institutions and government. In short, money market is a place where the demand for and supply of short term funds are met.

The **Capital Market** is the sector of the financial market where long-term financial instruments issued by corporations and governments trade. Here "long-term" refers to a financial instrument with an original maturity greater than one year and perpetual securities (those with no maturity). There are two types of capital market securities: those that represent shares of ownership interest, also called **Equity,** issued by corporations, and those that represent indebtedness, or **Debt** issued by corporations and by the state and local governments.

Financial markets can be classified in terms of:

a)  Cash Market and
b)  Derivative Markets.

The **Cash Market**, also referred to as the **Spot Market**, is the market for the immediate purchase and sale of a financial instrument.

In contrast, some financial instruments are contracts that specify that the contract holder has either the obligation or the choice to buy or sell another something at or by some future date. The "something" that is the subject of the contract is called the underlying (asset). The underlying asset is a stock, a bond, a financial index, an interest rate, a currency, or a commodity. Because the price of such contracts derive their value from the value of the underlying assets, these contracts are called **Derivative Instruments** and the market where they are traded is called the **derivatives market**.

*Classification on the Basis of Seasoning of Claim*

On this basis, financial markets are classified into primary market and secondary market.

**Primary market:** When a financial instrument is first issued, it is sold in the **Primary Market**. Primary markets are those markets which deal in the new securities. Therefore, they are also known as new issue markets. These are markets where securities are issued for the first time. In other words, these are the markets for the securities issued directly by the companies. The primary markets mobilise savings and supply fresh or additional capital to business units. In short, primary market is a market for raising fresh capital in the form of shares and debentures.

**Secondary market:** A **Secondary Market** is such in which financial instruments are resold among investors. No new capital is raised by the issuer of the security. Secondary markets are those markets which deal in existing securities. Existing securities are those securities that have already been issued and are already outstanding. Secondary market consists of stock exchanges. Stock exchanges are self regulatory bodies under the overall regulatory purview of the Govt. /SEBI.

Trading takes place among investors. Secondary markets are also classified in terms of:

a)  Organized stock exchanges and
b)  Over-the counter (OTC) markets.

**Organised Stock Exchanges** are central trading locations where financial instruments are traded.

**OTC Market** is generally where unlisted financial instruments are traded.

*Classification on the Basis of Structure or Arrangements*

On this basis, financial markets can be classified into organised markets and unorganized markets.

**Organised markets:** These are financial markets in which financial transactions take place within the well established exchanges or in the systematic and orderly structure.

**Unorganised markets:** These are financial markets in which financial transactions take place outside the well established exchange or without systematic and orderly structure or arrangements.

*Classification on the Basis of Timing of Delivery*

On this basis, financial markets may be classified into cash/spot market and forward/future market.

**Cash/Spot market:** This is the market where the buying and selling of commodities happens or stocks are sold for cash and delivered immediately after the purchase or sale of commodities or securities.

**Forward/Future market:** This is the market where participants buy and sell stocks/commodities, contracts and the delivery of commodities or securities occurs at a pre-determined time in future.

**Other types of financial market:** Apart from the above, there are some other types of financial markets. They are foreign exchange market and derivatives market.

**Foreign exchange market:** Foreign exchange market is simply defined as a market in which one country's currency is traded for another country's currency. It is a market for the purchase and sale of foreign currencies.

**Derivatives market:** The derivatives are most modern financial instruments in hedging risk. The individuals and firms who wish to avoid or reduce risk can deal with the others who are willing to accept the risk for a price. A common place where such transactions take place is called the derivative market. It is a market in which derivatives are traded. In short, it is a market for derivatives. The important types of derivatives are forwards, futures, options, swaps, etc.

## Capital Market

The capital market is a market for financial assets which have a long or indefinite maturity. Generally, it deals with long term securities which have a maturity period of more than one year. Capital market may be further divided into three types namely:

1.  Industrial Securities Market
2.  Government Securities Market and
3.  Long-term Loans Market.

*1.  Industrial Securities Market*

As the very name implies, it is a market for industrial securities, namely:

(i)  Equity shares.
(ii)  Preference shares and
(iii) Debentures or bonds.

It is a market where industrial concerns raise their capital or debt by issuing appropriate instruments. It can be further subdivided into two types. They are:

1.  Primary market or New Issue Market.
2.  Secondary market or Stock Exchange.

*2.  Government Securities Market*

It is otherwise called Gilt-Edged Securities Market. It is a market where government securities are traded. In India there are many kinds of Government securities-short term and long term. Long-term securities are traded in this market while short term securities are traded in money market. The secondary market for these securities is very narrow since most of the institutional investors tend to retain these securities until maturity.

*3.  Long-term Loans Market*

Development banks and commercial banks play a significant role in this market by supplying long term loans to corporate customers. Long term loans market may further be classified into:

(i)  Term loans,
(ii)  Mortgages and
(iii) Financial Guarantees markets.

## Money Market

Money market is a very important segment of a financial system. It is the market for dealing in monetary assets of short-term nature. Short-term funds up to one year and financial assets that are close substitutes for money are dealt in the money market. Money market instruments have the characteristics of liquidity (quick conversion into money), minimum transaction cost and no loss in value. Excess funds are deployed in the money market, which in turn is availed of to meet temporary shortages of cash and other obligations. Money market provides access to providers and users of short-term funds to fulfill their investments and borrowings requirements respectively at an efficient market clearing price. It performs the crucial role of providing an equilibrating mechanism to even out short-term liquidity, surpluses and deficits and in the process, facilitates the conduct of monetary policy. The money market is one of the primary mechanism through which the Central Bank influences liquidity and the general level of interest rates in an economy.

## Meaning of Money Market

A money market is a market for borrowing and lending of short-term funds. It deals in funds and financial instruments having a maturity period of one day to one year. It is a mechanism through which short-term funds are loaned or borrowed and through which a large part of financial transactions of a particular country or of the world are cleared.

It is different from stock market. It is not a single market but a collection of markets for several instruments like call money market, Commercial bill market etc. The Reserve Bank of India is the most important constituent of Indian money market. Thus RBI describes money market as "the centre for dealings, mainly of a short-term character, in monetary assets, it meets the short-term requirements of borrowers and provides liquidity or cash to lenders".

## Role of Money Market in Economy

Money markets play a key role in banks' liquidity management and the transmission of monetary policy. In normal times, money markets are among the most liquid in the financial sector. By providing the appropriate instruments and partners for liquidity trading, the money market allows the refinancing of short and medium-term positions and facilitates the mitigation of the business' liquidity risk.

The banking system and the money market represent the exclusive setting monetary policy operates in. A developed, active and efficient interbank market enhances the efficiency of central bank's monetary policy, transmitting its impulses into the economy best. Thus, the development of the money market smoothes the progress of financial intermediation and boosts lending to economy, hence improving the country's economic and social welfare. Therefore, the development of the money market is in all stakeholders' interests: the banking system elf, the Central Bank and the economy on the whole.

## Players of Money Market

In money market transactions of large amount and high volume take place. It is dominated by small number of large players. In money market the players are :-Government, RBI, DFHI (Discount and finance House of India) Banks, Mutual Funds, Corporate Investors, Provident Funds, PSUs (Public Sector Undertakings), NBFCs (Non-Banking Finance Companies) etc. The role and level of participation by each type of player differs from that of others.

## Functions of Money Markets

Due to short maturity term, the instruments of money market are liquid and can be converted to cash easily and thus are able to address the need of the short term surplus fund of the lenders and short term borrowing requirements of the borrowers. Thus, the major function of the money markets is to cater to the short term financial needs of the economy.

1. It caters to the short-term financial needs of the economy.
2. It helps the RBI in effective implementation of monetary policy.
3. It provides mechanism to achieve equilibrium between demand and supply of short-term funds.
4. It helps in allocation of short term funds through inter-bank transactions and money market instruments.
5. It also provides funds in non-inflationary way to the government to meet its deficits.
6. It facilitates economic development.
7. It helps in maintaining liquidity in the economy

## Features of Money Market

i. It is one market but collection of markets, such as, call money, notice money, repose, term money, treasury bills, commercial bills, certificate of deposits, commercial papers, inter-bank participation certificates, inter-corporate deposits, swaps futures, options, etc. and is concerned to deal in particular type of assets, the chief characteristic is its relative liquidity. All the sub-markets have close inter-relationship and free movement of funds from one sub-market to another. There has to be network of large number of participants which will add greater depth to the market.

ii. The activities in the money market tend to concentrate in some centre which serves a region or an area; the width of such area may vary considerably in some markets like London and New York which have become world financial centres. Where more than one Money Market operations market exists in a country, with screen-based trading and revolutions in information technology, such markets have rapidly becoming integrated into a national market. In India, Mumbai is emerging as a national market for money market instruments.

iii. The relationship that characterises a money market should be impersonal in character so that competition will be relatively pure.

iv. In a true money market, price differentials for assets of similar type (counterparty, maturity and liquidity) will tend to be eliminated by the interplay of demand and supply. Even for similar types of assets, some differential will no doubt continue to exist at any given point of time which gives scope for arbitrage.

v. Due to greater flexibility in the regulatory framework, there are constant endeavours for introducing new instruments/innovative dealing techniques;

vi. It is a wholesale market and the volume of funds or financial assets traded in the market are very large.

vii. The Indian money market has a dichotomic structure. It has a simultaneous existence of both the organized money market as well as unorganised money markets.

viii. The organised money market consists of RBI, all scheduled commercial banks and other recognised financial institutions. However, the unorganised part of the money market comprises domestic money lenders, indigenous bankers, trader, etc. The organised money market is in full control of the RBI. However, unorganised money market remains outside the RBI control.

ix. The demand for money in Indian money market is of a seasonal nature. India being an agriculture predominant economy, the demand for money is generated from the agricultural operations. During the busy season i.e. between October and April more agricultural activities takes place leading to a higher demand for money.

x. In the Indian money market, the organized bill market is not prevalent. Though the RBI tried to introduce the Bill Market Scheme (1952) and then New Bill Market Scheme in 1970, still there is no properly organized bill market in India.

xi. In our money market the supply of various instruments such as the Treasury Bills, Commercial Bills, Certificate of Deposits, Commercial Papers, etc. is very limited. In order to meet the varied requirements of borrowers and lenders, it is necessary to develop numerous instruments.

## Functions of a Developed Money Market

A well-developed money market is essential for a modern economy. Though, historically, money market has developed as a result of industrial and commercial progress, it also has important role to play in the process of industrialization and economic development of a country.

### 1. Financing Trade

Money Market plays crucial role in financing both internal as well as international trade. Commercial finance is made available to the traders through bills of exchange, which are discounted by the bill market. The acceptance houses and discount markets help in financing foreign trade.

### 2. Financing Industry

Money market contributes to the growth of industries in two ways:

a. Money market helps the industries in securing short-term loans to meet their working capital requirements through the system of finance bills, commercial papers, etc.

b. Industries generally need long-term loans, which are provided in the capital market. However, capital market depends upon the nature of and the conditions in the money market. The short-term interest rates of the money market influence the long-term interest rates of the capital market. Thus, money market indirectly helps the industries through its link with and influence on long-term capital market.

## 3. *Profitable Investment*

Money market enables the commercial banks to use their excess reserves in profitable investment. The main objective of the commercial banks is to earn income from its reserves as well as maintain liquidity to meet the uncertain cash demand of the depositors. In the money market, the excess reserves of the commercial banks are invested in near-money assets (e.g. short-term bills of exchange) which are highly liquid and can be easily converted into cash. Thus, the commercial banks earn profits without losing liquidity.

## 4. *Self-Sufficiency of Commercial Bank*

Developed money market helps the commercial banks to become self-sufficient. In the situation of emergency, when the commercial banks have scarcity of funds, need not approach the central bank and borrow at a higher interest rate. On the other hand, they can meet their requirements by recalling their old short-run loans from the money market.

## 5. *Help to Central Bank*

Though the central bank can function and influence the banking system in the absence of a money market, the existence of a developed money market smoothens the functioning and increases the efficiency of the central bank. Money market helps the central bank in two ways:

    a.    The short-run interest rates of the money market serves as an indicator of the monetary and banking conditions in the country and, in this way, guide the central bank to adopt an appropriate banking policy,

    b.    The sensitive and integrated money market helps the central bank to secure quick and widespread influence on the sub-markets, and thus achieve effective implementation of its policy.

## Components, Sub Markets of Indian Money Market

After studying above organisational chart of the Indian money market it is necessary to understand various components or sub markets within it. They are explained below.

1. **Call Money Market**: It an important sub market of the Indian money market. It is also known as money at call and money at short notice. It is also called inter bank loan market. In this market money is demanded for extremely short period. The duration of such transactions is from few hours to 14 days. It is basically located in the industrial and commercial locations such as Mumbai, Delhi, Calcutta, etc. These transactions help stock brokers and dealers to fulfill their financial requirements. The rate at which money is made available is called as a call rate. Thus rate is fixed by the market forces such as the demand for and supply of money.

2. **Commercial Bill Market**: Commercial bills market is basically a market of instruments similar to Bill of Exchange. The participants of commercial bill market in India are banks and financial institutions but this market is not yet developed. It is a market for the short term, self liquidating and negotiable money market instrument. Commercial bills are used to finance the movement and storage of agriculture and industrial goods in domestic and foreign markets. The commercial bill market in India is still underdeveloped.

3. **Treasury Bill Market**: This is a market for sale and purchase of short term government securities. These securities are called as Treasury Bills which are promissory notes or financial bills issued by the RBI on behalf of the Government of India. There are two types of treasury bills. (i) Ordinary or Regular Treasury Bills and (ii) Ad Hoc Treasury Bills. The maturity period of these securities range from as low as 14 days to as high as 364 days. They have become very popular recently due to high level of safety involved in them.

4. **Market for Certificate of Deposits (CDs)**: Certificate of Deposit (CD) refers to a money market instrument, which is negotiable and equivalent to a promissory note. All scheduled commercial banks excluding Regional Rural Banks (RRBs) and Local Area Banks (LABs) and Select All India Financial Institutions permitted by RBI are eligible to issue certificates of deposits. It is again an important segment of the Indian money market. The certificate of deposits is issued by the commercial banks. They are worth the value of Rs. 25 lakh and in multiple of Rs. 25 lakh. The minimum subscription of CD should be worth Rs. 1 Crore. The maturity period of CD is as low as 3 months and as high as 1 year. These are the transferable investment instrument in a money market. The government initiated a market of CDs in order to widen the range of instruments in the money market and to provide a higher flexibility to investors for investing their short term money.

5. **Market for Commercial Papers (CPs)**: Commercial Paper (CP) is yet another money market instrument in India, which was first introduced in 1990 to enable the highly rated corporate to diversify their resources for short term fund requirements. It is the market where the commercial papers are traded. Commercial paper (CP) is an investment instrument which can be issued by a listed company having working capital more than or equal to Rs. 5 cr. The CPs can be issued in multiples of Rs. 25 lakhs. However the minimum subscription should at least be Rs. 1 cr. The maturity period for the CP is minimum of 3 months and maximum 6 months. This was introduced by the government in 1990.

6. **Short Term Loan Market**: It is a market where the short term loan requirements of corporates are met by the Commercial banks. Banks provide short term loans to corporates in the form of cash credit or in the form of overdraft. Cash credit is given to industrialists and overdraft is given to businessmen.

7. **Money Market Mutual Funds (MMMFs):** Money Market Mutual Funds (MMMFs) were introduced by RBI in 1992 but since 2000, they are brought under the purview of the SEBI. They provide additional short-term avenue to individual investors. The Repo/Reverse Repo Market Repo (repurchase agreement) was introduced in December 1992. Repo means selling a security under an agreement to repurchase it at a predetermined date and rate. Repo transactions are affected between banks and financial institutions and among bank themselves, RBI also undertake Repo. IN 1996, Reverse Repo was introduced. Reverse Repo means buying a security on a spot basis with a commitment to resell on a forward basis. Reverse Repo transactions are affected with scheduled commercial banks and primary dealers.

8. **Discount and Finance House of India (DFHI):** It was established in 1988 by RBI and is jointly owned by RBI, public sector banks and all India financial institutions which have contributed to its paid up capital. DFHI plays important role in developing an active secondary market in Money Market Instruments. From 1996, it has been assigned status of a Primary Dealer (PD). It deals in treasury bills, commercial bills, CDs, CPs, short term deposits, call money market and government securities.

## Monetary Policy of India

Monetary policy is a regulatory policy by which the central bank or monetary authority of a country controls the supply of money, availability of bank credit and cost of money, that is, the rate of Interest.

Monetary policy/monetary management are regarded as an important tool of economic management in India. RBI controls the supply of money and bank credit. The Central bank has the duty to see that legitimate credit requirements are met and at the same credit is not used for unproductive and speculative purposes. RBI rightly calls its credit policy as one of controlled expansion.

**Objectives of Monetary Policy of India**

The main objective of monetary policy in India is 'growth with stability'. Monetary Management regulates availability, cost and use of money and credit. It also brings institutional changes in the financial sector of the economy. Following are the main objectives of monetary policy in India:

*1.  Growth with Stability*

Traditionally, RBI's monetary policy was focused on controlling inflation through contraction of money supply and credit. This resulted in poor growth performance. Thus, RBI has now adopted the policy of 'Growth with Stability'. This means sufficient credit will be available for growing needs of different sectors of economy and at the same time, inflation will be controlled with in a certain limit.

*2.  Regulation, Supervision and Development of Financial Stability*

Financial stability means the ability of the economy to absorb shocks and maintain confidence in financial system. Threats to financial stability can come from internal and external shocks. Such shocks can destabilize the country's financial system. Thus, greater importance is being given to RBI's role in maintaining confidence in financial system through proper regulation and controls, without sacrificing the objective of growth. Therefore, RBI is focusing on regulation, supervision and development of financial system.

*3.  Promoting Priority Sector*

Priority sector includes agriculture, export and small scale enterprises and weaker section of population. RBI with the help of bank provides timely and adequately credit at affordable cost of weaker sections and low income groups. RBI, along with NABARD, is focusing on microfinance through the promotion of Self Help groups and other institutions.

*4.  Generation of Employment*

Monetary policy helps in employment generation by influencing the rate of investment and allocation of investment among various economic activities of different labour Intensities.

*5.  External Stability*

With the growth of imports and exports India's linkages with global economy are getting stronger. Earlier, RBI controlled foreign exchange market by determining exchange rate. Now, RBI has only indirect control over external stability through the mechanism of 'managed Flexibility', where it influences exchange rate by buying and selling foreign currencies in open market.

*6.  Encouraging Savings and Investments*

RBI by offering attractive interest rates encourages savings in the economy. A high rate of saving promotes investment. Thus the monetary management by influencing rates of interest can influence saving mobilization in the country.

*7.  Redistribution of Income and Wealth*

By control of inflation and deployment of credit to weaker sectors of society the monetary policy may redistribute income and wealth favouring to weaker sections.

*8.  Regulation of NBFIs*

Non – Banking Financial Institutions (NBFIs), like UTI, IDBI, IFCI plays an important role in deployment of credit and mobilization of savings. RBI does not have any direct control on the functioning of such institutions. However it can indirectly affects the policies and functions of NBFIs through its monetary policy.

**Monetary Policy of RBI**

The Monetary Policy of RBI is not merely one of credit restriction, but it has also the duty to see that legitimate credit requirements are met and at the same time credit is not used for unproductive and speculative purposes RBI has various weapons of monetary control and by using them, it hopes to achieve its monetary policy.

## A. General

### a. Quantitative Credit Control Methods

In India, the legal framework of RBI's control over the credit structure has been provided under Reserve Bank of India Act, 1934 and the Banking Regulation Act, 1949. Quantitative credit controls are used to maintain proper quantity of credit o money supply in market. Some of the important general credit control methods are:

### 1. Bank Rate Policy

Bank rate is the rate at which the Central bank lends money to the commercial banks for their liquidity requirements. Bank rate is also called discount rate. In other words bank rate is the rate at which the central bank rediscounts eligible papers (like approved securities, bills of exchange, commercial papers etc) held by commercial banks.

Bank rate is important because it is the pace setter to other market rates of interest. Bank rates have been changed several times by RBI to control inflation and recession. By 2003, the bank rate has been reduced to 6% p.a.

### 2. Open Market Operations

It refers to buying and selling of government securities in open market in order to expand or contract the amount of money in the banking system. This technique is superior to bank rate policy. Purchases inject money into the banking system while sale of securities do the opposite. During last two decades the RBI has been undertaking switch operations. These involve the purchase of one loan against the sale of another or, vice-versa. This policy aims at preventing unrestricted increase in liquidity.

### 3. Cash Reserve Ratio (CRR)

The Gash Reserve Ratio (CRR) is an effective instrument of credit control. Under the RBI Act of, l934 every commercial bank has to keep certain minimum cash reserves with RBI. The RBI is empowered to vary the CRR between 3% and 15%. A high CRR reduces the cash for lending and a low CRR increases the cash for lending.

### 4. Statutory Liquidity Ratio (SLR)

Under SLR, the government has imposed an obligation on the banks to, maintain a certain ratio to its total deposits with RBI in the form of liquid assets like cash, gold and other securities. The RBI has power to  fix SLR in the range of 25% and 40% between 1990 and 1992 SLR was as high as 38.5%. Narasimham Committee did not favour maintenance of high SLR. The SLR was lowered down to 25% from 10ᵗʰOctober 1997.It was further reduced to 24% on November 2008. At present it is 25%.

### 5. Repo and Reverse Repo Rates

In determining interest rate trends, the repo and reverse repo rates are becoming important. Repo means Sale and Repurchase Agreement. Repo is a swap deal involving the immediate Sale of Securities and simultaneous purchase of those securities at a future date, at a predetermined price. Repo rate helps commercial banks to acquire funds from RBI by selling securities and also agreeing to repurchase at a later date. Reverse repo rate is the rate that banks get from RBI for parking their short term excess funds with RBI.

Repo and reverse repo operations are used by RBI in its Liquidity Adjustment Facility. RBI contracts credit by increasing the repo and reverse repo rates and by decreasing them it expands credit.

## B.  Selective / Qualitative Credit Control Methods

Under Selective Credit Control, credit is provided to selected borrowers for selected purpose, depending upon the use to which the controls try to regulate the quality of credit - the direction towards the credit flows. The Selective Controls are

### 1.  Ceiling on Credit

The Ceiling on level of credit restricts the lending capacity of a bank to grant advances against certain controlled securities.

### 2.  Margin Requirements

A loan is sanctioned against Collateral Security. Margin means that proportion of the value of security against which loan is not given. Margin against a particular security is reduced or increased in order to encourage or to discourage the flow of credit to a particular sector. It varies from 20% to 80%. For agricultural commodities it is as high as 75%. Higher the margin lesser will be the loan sanctioned.

### 3.  Discriminatory Interest Rate (DIR)

Through DIR, RBI makes credit flow to certain priority or weaker sectors by charging concessional rates of interest. RBI issues supplementary instructions regarding granting of additional credit against sensitive commodities, issue of guarantees, making advances etc.

### 4.  Directives

The RBI issues directives to banks regarding advances. Directives are regarding the purpose for which loans may or may not be given.

### 5.  Direct Action

It is too severe and is therefore rarely followed. It may involve refusal by RBI to rediscount bills or cancellation of license, if the bank has failed to comply with the directives of RBI.

### 6.  Moral Suasion

Under Moral Suasion, RBI issues periodical letters to bank to exercise control over credit in general or advances against particular commodities. Periodic discussions are held with authorities of commercial banks in this respect.

# 4. Credit Control

Credit control is an important tool used by Reserve Bank of India, a major weapon of the monetary policy used to control the demand and supply of money (liquidity) in the economy. Central Bank administers control over the credit that the commercial banks grant.

Such a method is used by RBI to bring "Economic Development with Stability". It means that banks will not only control inflationary trends in the economy but also boost economic growth which would ultimately lead to increase in real national income with stability.

## Need for Credit Control

Controlling Credit in the economy is amongst the most important functions of the Reserve Bank of India. The basic and important needs of credit control in the economy are-

- To encourage the overall growth of the *"priority sector"* i.e. those sectors of the economy which is recognized by the Government as "prioritized" depending upon their economic condition or government interest.
- To keep a check over the channelization of credit so that credit is not delivered for undesirable purposes.
- To achieve the objective of controlling inflation as well as deflation.
- To boost the economy by facilitating the flow of adequate volume of bank credit to different sectors.
- To develop the economy.

## Objectives of Credit Control

Credit control policy is just an arm of economic policy which comes under the purview of Reserve Bank of India, hence, its main objective being attainment of high growth rate while maintaining reasonable stability of the internal purchasing power of money. The broad objectives of credit control policy in India have been ensure an adequate level of liquidity enough to attain high economic growth rate along with maximum utilization of resource but without generating high inflationary pressure.

- Attain stability in exchange rate and money market of the country.
- Meeting the financial requirement during slump in the economy and in the normal times as well.
- Control business cycle and meet business needs.

## Methods of Credit Control

There are two methods that the RBI uses to control the money supply in the economy:

a) Qualitative method
b) Quantitative method

During the period of inflation Reserve Bank of India tightens its policies to restrict the money supply, whereas during deflation it allows the commercial bank to pump money in the economy.

## Qualitative Method

By *Quality* it is meant as the uses to which bank credit is directed. Qualitative method controls the manner of channelizing of cash and credit in the economy. It is a 'selective method' of control as it restricts credit for certain section where as expands for the other known as the 'priority sector' depending on the situation.

Tools used under this method are:

## 1. Marginal Requirement

Marginal requirement of loan = current value of security offered for loan-value of loans granted. The marginal requirement is increased for those business activities, the flow of whose credit is to be restricted in the economy. In case the flow of credit has to be increased, the marginal requirement will be lowered. RBI has been using this method since 1956.

E.g.: a person mortgages his property worth Rs. 100,000 against loan. The bank will give loan of Rs. 80,000 only. The marginal requirement here is 20%.

## 2. Rationing of Credit

Under this method there is a maximum limit to loans and advances that can be made, which the commercial banks cannot exceed. RBI fixes ceiling for specific categories. Such rationing is used for situations when credit flow is to be checked, particularly for speculative activities. Minimum of capital: total assets" (ratio between capital and total asset) can also be prescribed by Reserve Bank of India

## 3. Publicity

RBI uses media for the publicity of its views on the current market condition and its directions that will be required to be implemented by the commercial banks to control the unrest. Though this method is not very successful in developing nations due to high illiteracy existing making it difficult for people to understand such policies and its implications.

## 4. Direct Action

Under the Banking Regulation Act, the Central bank has the authority to take strict action against any of the commercial banks that refuses to obey the directions given by Reserve Bank of India. There can be a restriction on advancing of loans imposed by Reserve Bank of India on such banks.

E.g.: RBI had put up certain restrictions on the working of the Metropolitan co-operative banks. Also the 'Bank of Karad' had to come to an end in 1992.

## 5. Moral Persuasion

This method is also known as "moral persuasion" as the method that the Reserve Bank of India, being the apex bank uses here, is that of persuading the commercial banks to follow its directions/orders on the flow of credit. RBI puts a pressure on the commercial banks to put a ceiling on credit flow during inflation and be liberal in lending during deflation.

# 5. CENTRAL BANK

## Introduction

The Central Bank, as the ultimate monetary institution, reflects the monetary policy, and thereby a wider economic sovereignty of a country. In this respect, the definition of the central bank character, its functions and objectives is the primary task of every country. Although most central banks, from their very foundation, focused on ensuring financial stability, after the inflationary seventies, almost all of Central Banks set the price stability as the primary goal of their monetary policy. Of course, the preference for price stability does not challenge other objectives of economic policy, such as employment, economic growth and balance of payments equilibrium. On the contrary, the view is prevailing that the greatest contribution to these goals is provided precisely by maintaining macroeconomic stability.

## Meaning

In every country, there is one apex institution which acts as the leader of the money market. In supervises, regulates and controls are activities of commercial banks and other financial institutions. Such an institution is called as the central bank of the country. In India, RBI acts as a central Bank of the country.

Central Bank, as the ultimate monetary institution in the financial system of a country, is striving to provide optimum monetary conditions for the economic system functioning, while performing the functions of monetary regulation, supervision and the lender of last resort of banks. Sustaining monetary stability as the goal of monetary regulation function, and financial stability as the goal of supervision and lender-of-last-resort function, imposes the need to consider the possibilities for optimization of these functions, in the direction of simultaneously achieving price and financial stability.

## Functions

There are nine important functions of a central Bank. They are:

### 1. *Issue of Currency*

The central bank is given the sole monopoly of issuing currency in order to secure control over volume of currency and credit. These notes circulate throughout the country as legal tender money. It has to keep a reserve in the form of gold and foreign securities as per statutory rules against the notes issued by it.

It may be noted that RBI issues all currency notes in India except one rupee note. Again, it is under the directions of RBI that one rupee notes and small coins are issued by government mints. Remember, the central government of a country is usually authorised to borrow money from the central bank.

When the central government expenditure exceeds government revenue and the government is unable to reduce its expenditure, then it borrows from the RBI. This is done by selling security bills to RBI which creates new currency notes for the purpose. This is called monetisation of budget deficit or deficit financing. The government spends new currency and puts it into circulation to meet its expenditure.

### 2. *Banker to Government*

Central bank functions as a banker to the government-both central and state governments. It carries out all banking business of the government. Government keeps their cash balances in the current account with the central bank. Similarly, central bank accepts receipts and makes payment on behalf of the governments.

Also, central bank carries out exchange, remittance and other banking operations on behalf of the government. Central bank gives loans and advances to governments for temporary periods, as and when necessary and it also manages the public debt of the country. Remember, the central government can borrow any amount of money from RBI by selling its rupees securities to the latter.

### 3. Banker's Bank and Supervisor

There are usually hundreds of banks in a country. There should be some agency to regulate and supervise their proper functioning. This duty is discharged by the central bank.

### Central Bank Acts as Banker's Bank in Three Capacities

(i) It is the custodian of their cash reserves. Banks of the country are required to keep a certain percentage of their deposits with the central bank; and in this way the central bank is the ultimate holder of the cash reserves of commercial banks,

(ii) Central bank is lender of last resort. Whenever banks are short of funds, they can take loans from the central bank and get their trade bills discounted. The central bank is a source of great strength to the banking system,

(iii) It acts as a bank of central clearance, settlements and transfers. Its moral persuasion is usually very effective so far as commercial banks are concerned.

### 4. Controller of Credit and Money Supply

Central bank controls credit and money supply through its monetary policy which consists of two parts-currency and credit. Central bank has monopoly of issuing notes (except one-rupee notes, one-rupee coins and the small coins issued by the government) and thereby can control the volume of currency.

The main objective of credit control function of central bank is price stability along with full employment (level of output). It controls credit and money supply by adopting quantitative and qualitative measures. Following three quantitative measures of credit control by RBI are recalled for ready reference.

### Instruments of Money Policy

### i. Bank Rate (02009, 10C)

This is the rate of interest at which the central bank lends to commercial banks. It is, in a way, cost of borrowing. Cheap credit promotes investment whereas dear money discourages it. In a situation of excess demand and inflationary pressure, central bank increases the bank rate. High bank rate forces the commercial banks to raise, in turn, the rate of interest which makes credit dear. As a result, demand for loans and other purposes falls. Thus, increase in bank rate by the central bank adversely affects credit creation by commercial banks.

### ii. Open Market Operations

These refer to buying and selling of government securities by central bank to public and banks. This is done to influence money supply in the country. Mind, sale of government securities to commercial banks means flow of money into the central bank which reduces cash reserves. Consequently, credit availability of commercial banks is curtailed or controlled. When central bank buys securities, it increases cash reserves of the banks and their ability to give credit.

*iii.    Cash Reserve Ratio (CRR)*

Commercial banks are required under the law to keep a certain percentage of their total deposits with the central bank in the form of cash reserves. This is called CRR. It is a powerful instrument to control credit and lending capacity of the banks. To curtail the credit giving capacity of the banks, central bank raises the CRR but when it wants to enhance the credit giving powers of the bank, it reduces the CRR. Similarly, there is another measure called Legal Reserve Ratio which has two components like CRR and SLR. According to Statutory Liquidity Ratio or SLR, every bank is required to keep a fixed percentage (ratio) of its assets in cash called liquidity ratio. SLR is raised to reduce the ability of the banks to give credit. But SLR is reduced when the situation in the economy demands expansion of credit.

## 5.  Exchange Control

Another duty of a central bank is to see that the external value of currency is maintained. For instance, in India, the Reserve Bank of India takes steps to ensure external value of a rupee. It adopts suitable measures to attain this object. The exchange control system is one such measure.

Under exchange control system, every citizen of India has to deposit with the Reserve Bank of India all foreign currency or exchange that he receives. And whatever foreign exchange he might need has to be secured from the Reserve Bank by making an application in the prescribed form.

## 6.  Lender of Last Resort

When commercial banks have exhausted all resources to supplement their funds at times of liquidity crisis, they approach central bank as a last resort. As lender of last resort, central bank guarantees solvency and provides financial accommodation to commercial banks (i) by rediscounting their eligible securities and bills of exchange and (ii) by providing loans against their securities. This saves banks from possible failure and banking system from a possible breakdown. On the other hand, central bank, by providing temporary financial accommodation, saves the financial structure of the country from collapse.

## 7.  Custodian of Foreign Exchange or Balances

It has been mentioned above that a central bank is the custodian of foreign exchange reserves and nation's gold. It keeps a close watch on external value of its currency and undertakes exchange management control. All the foreign currency received by the citizens has to be deposited with the central bank; and if citizens want to make payment in foreign currency, they have to apply to the central bank. Central bank also keeps gold and bullion reserves.

## 8.  Clearing House Function

Banks receive cheques drawn on the other banks from their customers which they have to realise from drawee banks. Similarly, cheques on a particular bank are drawn and passed into the hands of other banks which have to realise them from the drawee banks. Independent and separate realisation to each cheque would take a lot of time and, therefore, central bank provides clearing facilities, i.e., facilities for banks to come together every day and set off their chequing claims.

## 9.  Collection and Publication of Data

It has also been entrusted with the task of collection and compilation of statistical information relating to banking and other financial sectors of the economy.

# 6. BANKING SYSTEMS

## Introduction to Banking Systems

Banking system plays a very significant part in the economy of a country. It is central to a nation's financial system as it caters to the needs of credit for all the sections of the society. Money-lending in one structure has evolved along with the history of mankind. Reserve Bank of India was set up to regulate the formal banking sector in the country. Ever since the banks were nationalized in 1969, banks have been playing a major role in the socio-economic life of the country. India is not only the world's largest independent democracy, but also an emerging economic colossal. For the past three decades, India's banking system has several outstanding achievements to its credit. Most of the credit-related schemes of the government to uplift the poorer and the under-privileged sections have been implemented through the banking sector. With the passing of the Reserve Bank of India Act 1934, there were improvements in agricultural credit. The government has allocated Rs.10000 crore to the National Bank for Agriculture and Rural Development (NABARD) for refinancing Regional Rural Banks (RRBs) to disburse short term crop loans to small and marginal farmers. The short-term crop loans scheme offers credit to farmers at 7 per cent interest rate. Besides, in order to reduce post-harvest losses, farmers are eligible to get post-harvest loans up to six months at 4 per cent interest rate provided the bank keep their produce in warehouses. The rural sector in a country like India can grow only if cheaper credit is available to the farmers for their short and medium-term loans. In addition, the farmers get loans for purchase of electric motors with pump, tractors and other machinery, digging wells or boring wells, purchase of dairy animals and for many other allied enterprises.

The Industrial Development Bank of India (IDBI) is the premier institution in India purveying financial assistance to the industrial sector projects. It provides direct financial assistance to the industrial concerns in the form of granting loans and advances, and purchasing or underwriting the issues of stocks, bonds or debentures. The creation of the Development Assistance Fund is the special of the IDBI. The Fund is used to provide assistance to those industries which are not able to obtain funds mainly because of heavy investment involved or low expected rate of returns. Assistance from the Fund requires the prior approval by the government. Apart from this, the IDBI even gives guidance to start a business.

In addition to the above traditional roles, banks also perform certain new age functions which could not be thought of a couple of decades ago. Today, the banking sector is one of the biggest service sectors in India. Availability of quality services is vital for the well-being of the economy. The focus of banks has shifted from customer acquisition to customer retention. With the stepping in of information technology in the banking sector, the working strategy of the banking sector has been revolutionary changes. Various customer-oriented products like internet banking, ATM services, telebanking and electronic payment have lessened the workload of customers. The facility of internet banking enables a consumer to access and operate his bank account without actually visiting the bank premises. The facility of ATMs and credit/debit cards has revolutionized the choices available with the customers. Banks also serve as alternative gateways for making payments on account of income-tax and online payment of various bills like the telephone, electricity and tax. In the modern-day economy where people have not time to make these payments by standing in queue, the services provided by banks are commendable.

## Role of Banking in India's Developing Economy

One of the major considerations that led to the nationalization of the fourteen major commercial banks of India in 1969 was the fact that banks, in general, had been negligent of the vital priority sectors of the economy, viz., agriculture and small-scale industries. The commercial banks had remained largely indifferent to the credit needs of the farmers for agricultural operations and land improvement. A handful of people were able to exploit the bank finance to serve their own individual interests and convenience. Very often, the bank used bank funds for the hoarding of essential articles and for specialization, thus nurturing anti-social elements. Nationalization brought about a major policy shift in the working of these banks.

The economic development of our country depends more on real factors like the industrial development, modernization of agriculture, organization of internal trade and expansion of foreign trade, especially exports, and less on the monetary factors contributed by banking Economic planning like laying down of specific targets and allocating particular sums of money that constitute the economic policy of the government also plays a significant role. Still we cannot under-estimate the importance of banking and the monetary mechanism.

One of the most important problems of a developing economy is that of capital formation. There is a good deal of difference between hoarding and saving and the people in the countryside have to be made to realize the difference. This can be easily done by banks. The bank can undertake to educate the rural populace and thus mobilize their savings. A number of leading economists have confirmed the fact that the amount of capital available in India for investment is surprisingly and inexplicably large. Both in rural and urban areas, huge amounts of money are wasted on celebrations like marriages and births. If banks can offer handsome interest on savings, people can be induced to direct their savings from wasteful activities to banks. Promoting attractive deposit schemes needs some very active work on the part of the banks, but it can certainly mobilize a large amount of saving for capital formation.

The Government of India has now undertaken a large number of projects for the economic reconstruction of the country. Banks can generate an adequate volume of credit and conduct it along useful productive channels. The bank can distinguish between the essential and non-essential factors of the economy between productive and non-productive investment, between speculative arid non-speculative borrowing and thus help in the growth of the economy.

Two other acute problems faced by our low and middle income groups are the housing problem and gnawing unemployment problem. If the banks undertake to help these groups, the groups will also be making a significant contribution to our economy. It will also help in removing the economic imbalance of the various sections of our society.

Before nationalization, our banks could not play this constructive role expected of them. But after nationalization, the entire banking machinery has now been geared to the economic development of the country. The banks have started looking after the needs of the small farmer and the new entrepreneur. It is earnestly hoped that the Government will take some more positive steps to ensure that the real benefits of an organized banking system percolate down to the poor illiterate masses of India.

# 7. STATE BANK OF INDIA

## Introduction

The State Bank of India, popularly known as SBI, is one of the leading banks in India. The bank traces its origin to the first decade of the 19th century. Later on, it was merged with the Imperial Bank. In the year 1955, the Government of India nationalized the Imperial Bank along with the Reserve Bank of India. Ever since that time, the bank acquired its present name that is SBI.

## History

The evolution of State Bank of India can be traced back to the first decade of the 19th century. The origins of State Bank of India date back to 2 June 1806 when the Bank of Calcutta (later called the Bank of Bengal) was established. It was the first ever joint-stock bank of the British India, established under the sponsorship of the Government of Bengal. The bank was redesigned as the Bank of Bengal, three years later, on 2 January 1809.Subsequently, the Bank of Bombay (established on 15 April 1840) and the Bank of Madras (established on 1 July 1843) followed the Bank of Bengal. These three banks dominated the modern banking scenario in India, until when the banks were amalgamated to form the Imperial Bank of India, on 27 January1921. In 1921, the Bank of Bengal and two other banks (Bank of Madras and Bank of Bombay) were amalgamated to form the Imperial Bank of India.

The All India Rural Credit Survey Committee proposed the takeover of the Imperial Bank of India, and integrating with it, the former state-owned or state-associate banks. Subsequently, an Act was passed in the Parliament of India in May 1955. As a result, the State Bank of India (SBI) was established on 1 July 1955.

In 1955, the Reserve Bank of India acquired the controlling interests of the Imperial Bank of India and SBI was created by an act of Parliament to succeed the Imperial Bank of India. This resulted in making the State Bank of India more powerful, because as much as a quarter of the resources of the Indian banking system were controlled directly by the State. Later on, the State Bank of India (Subsidiary Banks) Act was passed in 1959. The Act enabled the State Bank of India to make the eight former State-associated banks as its subsidiaries.

State Bank of India, with a 200 year history, is the largest commercial bank in India in terms of assets, deposits, profits, branches, customers and employees. The bank has been striving sincerely to adhere to the efforts of providing supreme customer satisfaction to the best possible extent. The SBI has occurrence all over India with 16,000 branches. SBI created aexceptional method of serving its customers even on a holiday. The Government of India is the single largest shareholder of this Fortune 500 entity with 58.60% ownership. SBI is ranked 59th in the list of 'Top 1000 World Banks 2015' by The Banker magazine. CurrentlySBI ATM is being floated on a boat in the backwaters of Kerala. This caters to the needs of the customers by providing service round the clock. Besides, the customers can also avail the facilities of online banking and transactions.

## Functions

The State Bank of India performs all the functions of a commercial bank and acts as an agent of the Reserve Bank in those places were the RBI has no branch offices. Accordingly, it renders the following functions:

## A. Central Banking Functions

It acts as the agent of the Reserve Bank in all those places where the RBI does not have its own branches.

The State Bank of India acts as an agent of the Reserve Bank of India and performs the following functions:

*1. Acts as the Bankers Bank*

- Receives deposits from the commercial banks
- Grants loans to the commercial banks on demand.
- Rediscounts the bills of the commercial banks.
- Acts as the clearing-house for the other commercial banks.

*2. Acts as the Government's Banker*

It collects money from the public on behalf of the government and also makes payments. The bank also manages the public debt of the Central and the State Governments.

*3. Remittance*

The State Bank of India facilitates remittance of money from one place to another. It helps in the transfer on the funds of the State and Central Government.

## B. Ordinary Banking Functions

The ordinary banking functions of the State Bank are as follows:

1. **Receiving Deposits from the Public:** The State Bank receives different types of deposits from the public for example Fixed Deposits, Recurring Deposits Saving Account and Current Accounts.
2. **Investment in Securities**: Like other commercial banks, the State Bank invests its surplus funds in the Securities of Government of India, the State Governments, Railway Securities, Securities of Corporations and Treasury Bills.
3. **Loans and Advances:** The State Bank grants loans and advances to people against the approved security. It lends money to merchants and manufacturers for short periods. It also lends to farmers and co-operative institutions. It lends mostly on the security of easily realizable commodities like rice, wheat, cotton, oil-seeds, cloth, gold and government securities. The Bank can lend against agricultural bills upto a maximum period of fifteen months and incase of other bills upto a maximum period of six months.
4. **Subsidiary Functions**: The State Bank performs various subsidiary services also. It collects checks, drafts, bill of exchange, dividends interest, salaries and pensions on behalf of its customers. It purchases and sells securities on behalf of its customer. It receives valuables and documents for safe custody and maintains safe deposit vaults.

## C. Prohibited Functions of the SBI

1. The State Bank of India Act has enumerated certain business which cannot be done by the State Bank.
2. The State Bank cannot grant loans against stocks and shares for a period exceeding Six months.
3. The State Bank can purchase no immovable property except for its own offices.
4. The State Bank cannot re-discount those bills which do not carry at least two good signatures.
5. The State Bank could neither discount bills nor extends credit to individuals or firms above the sanctioned limit.
6. The State Bank can neither re-discount nor offer loans against the security of those exchange bills whose period of maturity exceeds six months.

## Associate Banks of SBI

SBI has five associate banks & its associates Banks are governed under State Bank of India (Subsidiary Banks) Act, 1959. All Associates of SBI Use the State Bank of India logo, which is a blue circle, and all use the "State Bank of" name, followed by the regional headquarters' name:

- State Bank of Bikaner & Jaipur
- State Bank of Hyderabad
- State Bank of Mysore
- State Bank of Patiala
- State Bank of Travancore

Earlier SBI had seven associate banks. State Bank of Saurashtra and State Bank of Indore merged with SBI on 13 August 2008 and 19 June 2009 respectively.

**Non-Banking Subsidiaries**: Apart from its five associate banks, SBI also has the following nonbanking subsidiaries:

- SBI Capital Markets Ltd
- SBI Funds Management Pvt Ltd
- SBI Factors & Commercial Services Pvt Ltd
- SBI Cards & Payments Services Pvt. Ltd. (SBICPSL)
- SBI DFHI Ltd
- SBI Life Insurance Company Limited
- SBI General Insurance

# 8. Co-operative Banks

Co-operative banking is retail and commercial banking organized on a co-operative basis. Co-operative banking institutions take deposits and lend money in most parts of the world. Co-operative banking includes retail banking carried out by credit unions, mutual savings banks, building societies and co-operatives, as well as commercial banking services provided by mutual organizations to co-operative businesses.

## Introduction

Co-operative Banks in India have become an integral part of the success of Indian Financial Inclusion story. The banks have achieved many landmarks since their conception and have helped a normal rural Indian to believe empowered and secure. In India, there is anoverabundanceof banks providing almost all services that an individual requires. But most of the banks that people use are either private or nationalised banks. However, there is another sector of banks that is used by a large number of the middle class sections of the society co-operative banks. Though much smaller as compared to scheduled commercial banks, co-operative banks constitute an important segment of the Indian banking system. The banks have an extensive branch network and reach out to people in remote areas. The banks have traditionally played an important role in creating banking habits among the lower and middle-income groups and in strengthening the rural credit delivery system. Co-operative banks are small-sized units organized in the co-operative sector which operate both in urban and non-urban centers. These banks are traditionally centered on communities, localities and work place groups and the banks essentially lend to small borrowers and businesses.

In India Co operative Banks are registered under the Co-operative Societies Act. The co-operative bank is also regulated by the RBI. The banks are governed by the Banking Regulations Act 1949 and Banking Laws (Co-operative Societies) Act, 1965. These banks provide most services such as savings and current accounts, safe deposit lockers, loan or mortgages to private and business customers and for middle class users for saving their money.

Co-operative banks are a vital part of the Indian financial system. Thebank encompass urban co-operative banks and rural co-operative credit institutions. Co-operative banks in India are more than 100 years old. Urban Co-operative Banks also referred to as primary co-operative banksplay a significant role in meeting the growing credit needs of urban and sem-urban areas of the country. Urban Co-operative Banks mobilize savings from the middle and lower income groups and provide credit to small borrowers, including weaker sections of the society. Scheduled Urban Co-operative Banks are under closer regulatory and managerial framework of the RBI. Rural co-operative banks operate mainly for the benefit of rural areas, particularly the agricultural sector.

The Co-Operative Banks in rural areas mainly finance agricultural based activities including farming, cattle, milk, hatchery, personal finance, et cetera, along with some small scale industries and self-employment driven activities, the co-operative banks in urban areas mainly finance various categories of people for self-employment, industries, small scale units and home finance. The Co-Operative Banking structure in India is divided into following main 5 categories:

- Primary Urban Co-op Banks
- Primary Agricultural Credit Societies
- District Central Co-op Banks
- State Co-operative Banks
- Land Development Banks

Co-operative banks function on the basis of 'no-profit no-loss'. Co-operative banks, as a principle, do not pursue the goal of profit maximisation. Therefore, these banks do not focus on offering more than the basic banking services. So, co-operative banks finance small borrowers in industrial and trade sectors, besides professional and salary classes. Although are not better than private banks in terms of facilities provided, their interest rates are definitely competitive.

However, unlike private banks, the documentation process is lengthy if not inflexible and getting a loan approved quickly is rather complex. The criteria for getting a loan from Co-operative banks are less rigid than for a loan from a commercial bank. So, it makes better sense to bank with Co-operative banks today, what with the rates some offer being the best in the industry. And with the risk of a run minimized, the banks are almost on an equal footing with commercial banks.

## History of Co-operative Banking in India

The historical roots of the Co-operative Movement in the world days back to days of gloom and misery in Europe faced by common people who had little or no access to credit to fund their basic needs, in uncertain times. The idea spread when the continent was faced with economic turmoil which led large populations to live at subsistence level without any economic security. People were forced to poverty and deprivation. It was the idea of Hermann Schulze (1808-83) and Friedrich Wilhelm Raiffeisen (1818-88) which took shape as co-operative banks of today across the world. The banks started to promote the idea of easy availability of credit to small businesses and for the poor segment of society. It was similar to the many microfinance institutions which have become highly popular in developing economies of today. Although this helped spread co-operative movement in many parts of Europe, in British Isles it is came from the revivalist Christian movement and found high acceptance with working class and lower middle class segments of society. However, UK and Irish credit unions in 20th century were inspired by US credit unions which in-turn owe their emergence to Canadian adaptations of the German co-operative banking concept. These movements were supported by governments of the respective countries. This success was achieved due to the failure of the commercial banks to fund and support the needs of small business owners and ordinary people who were outside the formal banking net. Co-operative banks helped overcome the vital market imperfections and serviced the poorer layers of society.

The Co-operative Credit Societies Act, 1904 led to the formation of Co-operative Credit Societies in both rural and urban areas. The act was based on recommendations of Sir Frederick Nicholson (1899) and Sir Edward Law (1901). The ideas in turn were based on the pattern of Raiffeisen and Schulze respectively. The Co-operative Societies Act of 1912, further gave recognition to the formation of non-credit societies and the central co-operative organizations.

## Features of Co-operative Bank

**Co-operative banks** are deeply rooted inside local areas and communities. The banks are involved in local development and contribute to the sustainable development of their communities, as their members and management board usually belong to the communities in which the banks exercise their activities. By increasing banking access in areas or markets where other banks are less present SMEs, farmers in rural areas, middle or low income households in urban areas co-operative banks reduce banking exclusion and foster the economic ability of millions of people.The bank play an influential role on the economic growth in the countries in which the banks work in and increase the efficiency of the international financial system. Their specific form of enterprise, relying on the above mentioned principles of organization, has proven successful both in developed and developing countries.

1. **Customer's Owned Entities**: In a co-operative bank, the needs of the customers meet the needs of the owners, as co-operative bank members are both. As a consequence, the first aim of a co-operative bank is not to maximise profit but to provide the best possible products and services to its members. Some co-operative banks only operate with their members but most of them also admit non-member clients to benefit from their banking and financial services.
2. **Democratic Member Control**: Co-operative banks are owned and controlled by their members, who democratically elect the board of directors. Members usually have equal voting rights, according to the co-operative principle of "one person, one vote".
3. **Profit Allocation**: In a co-operative bank, a significant part of the yearly profit, benefits or surplus is usually allocated to constitute reserves. A part of this profit can also be distributed to the co-operative members, with legal or statutory limitations in most cases. Profit is usually allocated to members either through a patronage dividend, which is related to the use of the co-operative's products and services by each member, or through an interest or a dividend, which is related to the number of shares subscribed by each member.

## Structure of Co-operative Banking in India

The structure of co-operative network in India can be divided into 2 broad segments:

- Urban Co-operative Banks
- Rural Co-operatives Urban Co-operatives

## Urban Co-operative Banks

Urban Co-operatives can be further divided into:

- Scheduled and
- Non-scheduled.

Both the categories are further divided into multi-state and single-state. Majority of these banks falls in the non-scheduled and single-state category. Banking activities of Urban Co-operative Banks are monitored by RBI. Registration and Management activities are managed by Registrar of Co-operative Societies. This Registrar of Co-operative Societies operates in single-state and Central Registrar of Co-operative Societiesoperates in multiple states.

## Rural Co-Operatives

The rural co-operatives are further divided into:

- Short-term and
- Long-term structures.

The *short-term co-operative banks* are three tiered operating in different states. These are:

- **State Co-operative Banks**: the banks operate at the apex level in states.
- **District Central Co-operative Banks**: the banks operate at the district levels.
- **Primary Agricultural Credit Societies**: the banks operate at the village or grass-root level.

The*Long-term structures*are further divided into:

- State Co-operative Agriculture and Rural Development Banks (SCARDS): These operate at state-level.
- Primary Co-operative Agriculture and Rural Development Banks (PCARDBS): The banks operate at district/block level.

The rural banking co-operatives have anintricate monitoring structure as the banks have a dual control which has led to many problems. A Forum called State Level Task Force on Co-operative Urban Banks (TAFCUB) has been set-up to look into issues related to duality in control. All banking activities are regulated by a shared arrangement between RBI and NABARD.

## Types of Co-operative Banks in India

The co-operative banks are small-sized units which operate both in urban and non-urban centers. The banks hey finance small borrowers in industrial and trade sectors besides professional and salary classes. Regulated by the Reserve Bank of India, are governed by the Banking Regulations Act 1949 and banking laws (co-operative societies) act, 1965. The co-operative banking structure in India is divided into five main categories:

### A.  Primary Co-operative Credit Society

The primary co-operative credit society is an association of borrowers and non-borrowers residing in a particular locality. The funds of the society are derived from the share capital and deposits of members and loans from central co-operative banks. The borrowing powers of the members as well as of the society are fixed. The loans are given to members for the purchase of cattle, fodder, fertilizers, pesticides, etc.

### B.  Central Co-operative Banks

These are the federations of primary credit societies in a district and are of two types-those having a membership of primary societies only and those having a membership of societies as well as individuals. The funds of the bank consist of share capital, deposits, loans and overdrafts from state co-operative banks and joint stocks. These banks provide finance to member societies within the limits of the borrowing capacity of societies. The banks also conduct all the business of a joint stock bank.

### C.  State Co-operative Banks

The state co-operative bank is a federation of central co-operative bank and acts as a watchdog of the co-operative banking structure in the state. Its funds are obtained from share capital, deposits, loans and overdrafts from the Reserve Bank of India. The state co-operative banks lend money to central co-operative banks and primary societies and not directly to the farmers.

### D.  Land Development Banks

The Land development banks are organized in 3 tiers namely; state, central, and primary level and the banks meet the long term credit requirements of the farmers for developmental purposes. The state land development banks oversee, the primary land development banks situated in the districts and tehsil areas in the state. The banks are governed both by the state government and Reserve Bank of India. Recently, the supervision of land development banks has been assumed by National Bank for Agriculture and Rural development (NABARD). The sources of funds for these banks are the debentures subscribed by both central and state government. These banks do not accept deposits from the general public.

### E.  Urban Co-operative Banks

The term Urban Co-operative Banks (UCBs), though not formally defined, refers to primary co-operative banks located in urban and semi-urban areas. These banks, till 1996, were allowed to lend money only for non-agricultural purposes. This distinction does not hold today. These banks were traditionally centered on communities, localities, work place groups. The banks essentially lend to small borrowers and businesses. Today, their scope of operations has widened considerably.

The origins of the urban co-operative banking movement in India can be traced to the secure of nineteenth century. Inspired by the victory of the experiments related to the co-operative movement in Britain and the co-operative credit movement in Germany, such societies were set up in India. Co-operative societies are based on the principles of cooperation, communal help, democratic decision making, and open membership. Co-operatives represented a new and alternative approach to organization as against proprietary firms, partnership firms, and joint stock companies which represent the foremost form of commercial organization. The bank mainly rely upon deposits from members and non-members and in case of need and get finance from either the district central co-operative bank to which the banks are affiliated or from the apex co-operative bank if the banks work in big cities where the apex bank has its Head Office. The banks provide credit to small scale industrialists, salaried employees, and other urban and semi-urban residents.

## Functions of Co-Operative Banks

Co-operative banks also perform the basic banking functions of banking but the banks differ from commercial banks in the following respects

1. Commercial banks are joint-stock companies under the companies' act of 1956, or public sector bank under a separate act of a parliament whereas co-operative banks were established under the co-operative society's acts of different states.
2. Commercial bank structure is branch banking structure whereas co-operative banks have a three tier setup, with state co-operative bank at apex level, central/district co-operative bank at district level, and primary co-operative societies at rural level.
3. Only some of the sections of banking regulation act of 1949 (fully applicable to commercial banks), are applicable to co-operative banks, resulting only in partial control by RBI of co-operative banks and
4. Co-operative banks function on the principle of cooperation and not entirely on commercial parameters.

## Differences between Co-Operative Banks and Commercial Banks in India

1. Commercial banks are joint-stock banks. Co-operatives banks, on the other hand, are co-operative organisations.
2. Commercial banks are governed by the Banking Regulation Act. Co-operative banks are governed by the Co-operative Societies Act of 1904.
3. Commercial banks are subject to the control of the Reserve Bank of India directly. Co-operative banks are subject to the rules laid down by the Registrar of Co-operative Societies.
4. Co-operative banks have lesser scope in offering a variety of banking services than commercial banks.
5. Commercial banks in India are on a larger scale. The banks have adopted the system of branch banking, so the banks have countrywide operations. Co-operative banks are relatively on a much smaller scale. Many co-operative banks follow only unit-bank system, though there are co-operative banks with a number of branches but their coverage is not countrywide.
6. Commercial banks in India are of two types:
    i.   Public sector banks and
    ii.  Private sector banks.
    Co-operative banks are private sector banks.
7. Commercial banks mostly provide short-term finance to industry, trade and commerce, including priority sectors like exports, etc.Co-operative banks usually cater to the credit needs of agriculturists.

8.  Co-operative banks offer a slightly higher rate of interest to their depositors than commercial banks.
9.  In co-operative banks, borrowers are member shareholders, so the banks have some influence on the lending policy of the banks, on account of their voting power.Borrowers of commercial banks are only account- holders and have no voting power as such, so the banks cannot have any influence on the lending policy of these banks.
10. Co-operative banks have not much scopeflexibility on account of the rigidities of the bye-laws of the Co-operative Societies. Commercial banks, on the other hand, are free from such rigidities.

# 9. National Bank for Agriculture and Rural Development (NABARD)

## Introduction

**National Bank for Agriculture and Rural Development** (NABARD) is a Development Bank with a mandate for providing and regulating credit and other facilities for the promotion and development of agriculture, small-scale industries, cottage and village industries, handicrafts and other rural crafts and other allied economic activities in rural areas with a view to promoting integrated rural development and securing prosperity of rural areas, and for matters connected therewith or incidental thereto.

NABARD is an apex development bank in India, having headquarters in Mumbai and other branches are all over the country. The Committee to Review Arrangements for Institutional Credit for Agriculture and Rural Development (CRAFICARD), set up by the Reserve Bank of India under the chairmanship of Shri B. Sivaraman, conceived and recommended the establishment of National Bank for Agriculture and Rural Development. NABARD's activities are governed by a Board of Directors. The Board of Directors is appointed by the Government of India in harmony with NABARD Act 1981. It was established on 12 July 1982 by a special Act of parliament and its main focus was on upliftment of rural India by increasing the credit flow for elevation of agriculture & rural non farm sector and completed its 34 years on 1 Jan 2016. It has been entrusted with "matters concerning policy, planning and operations in the field of credit for agriculture and other economic activities in rural areas in India". RBI sold its stake in NABARD to the Government of India, which now holds 99% stakeand RBI holds 1% (initially 72.5%) stake in NABARD. NABARD is active in developing financial inclusion policy and is a member of the Alliance for Financial Inclusion.

NABARD is designated as an apex development bank in the country.This national bank was established in 1982 by a Special Act of the Parliament, with a mandate to uplift rural India by facilitating credit flow in agriculture, cottage and village industries, handicrafts and small-scale industries. It is also required to support non-farm sector while promoting other allied economic activities in rural areas. NABARD functions to promote sustainable rural development for attaining prosperity of rural areas in India.

It is basically concerned with "matters concerning policy, as well as planning and operations in the field of credit for agriculture and other economic activities in rural areas in India". It is worth noting with reference to NABARD that RBI has sold its own stake to the Government of India. Therefore, Government of India holds 99% stake in NABARD.

## Objectives

More than 50% of the rural credit is disbursed by the Co-operative Banks and Regional Rural Banks. NABARD is responsible for regulating and supervising the functions of Co-operative banks and RRBs. NABARD works towards providing a strong and efficient rural credit delivery system, capable of taking care of the expanding and diverse credit needs of agriculture and rural development.

NABARD was established with an initial capital of 100 cr., on 12 July 1982 by a special act of parliament 1981, by transferring the agricultural credit functions of RBI and refinance functions of the then Agricultural Refinance and Development Corporation (ARDC). NABARD replaced the Agricultural Credit Department (ACD) and Rural Planning and Credit Cell (RPCC) of Reserve Bank of India, and Agricultural Refinance and Development Corporation (ARDC)

## Role of NABARD

1. It is an apex institution which has power to deal with all matters concerning policy, planning as well as operations in giving credit for agriculture and other economic activities in the rural areas.
2. It is a refinancing agency for those institutions that provide investment and production credit for promoting the several developmental programs for rural development.
3. It is improving the absorptive capacity of the credit delivery system in India, including monitoring, formulation of rehabilitation schemes, restructuring of credit institutions, and training of personnel.
4. It co-ordinates the rural credit financing activities of all sorts of institutions engaged in developmental work at the field level while maintaining liaison with Government of India, and State Governments, and also RBI and other national level institutions that are concerned with policy formulation.
5. It prepares rural credit plans, annually, for all districts in the country.
6. It also promotes research in rural banking, and the field of agriculture and rural development.

## Functions of NABARD

The full form of NABARD is National Bank for Agriculture and Rural Development. The major functions of NABARD are as follows:

*Major Functions*

1. NABARD gives high priority to projects formed under IRDP.
2. It provides refinance for IRDP accounts in order to give highest share for the support for poverty alleviation programs run by IRDP.
3. Other than the activities included under IRDP, it also makes the service area plan, to provide backward and forward linkages and also infrastructural support.
4. NABARD also prepares guidelines for promotion of group activities under its programs and provides 100% refinance support for them.
5. It is making efforts to establish linkages between Self-help Group (SHG) that are organized by voluntary agencies for poor and needy in rural areas and other official credit agencies.
6. It refinances to the complete extent for those projects that are taken under the 'National Watershed Development Programme and the 'National Mission of Wasteland Development'.
7. It also has a system of District Oriented Monitoring Studies, under which, study is conducted for a cross section of schemes that are sanctioned in a district to various banks, to ascertain their performance and to identify the constraints in their implementation, italso initiates appropriate action to remedy them.
8. It also supports Vikas volunteer Vahini programs which offer credit and development activities to poor farmers.
9. It also inspects and supervises the cooperative banks and RRBs to periodically ensure the development of the rural financing and farmers' welfare.
10. NABARAD also recommends about licensing for RRBs and Cooperative banks to RBI.
11. NABARD also provides assistance and support for the training and development of the staff of various other credit institutions that are engaged in credit distributions.
12. It also runs programs for agriculture and rural development.
13. It is engaged in regulations of the cooperative banks and the RRB's, and manages their talent acquisition through IBPS CWE conducted across the country.

14. It acts as an apex body for meeting the credit needs of all types of agricultural and rural development.
15. It provides refinancing facilities to State Co-operative Banks(SCBs), Land Development Bank (LDBs), Regional Rural Banks (RRBs) and other approved financial institutions for financing rural economic activities.
16. It co-ordinates all agricultural and rural development activities with the objective of tying them up with planned development activities in the rural sector.
17. It provides short-term, medium-term and long-term credit to SCBs, LDBs, RRBs and approved financial institutions.
18. It provides long-term assistance (not exceeding 20 years) to State Governments.
19. It has the responsibility of inspecting co-operative banks and RRBs.
20. It maintains a research and development fund to promote research in agriculture and rural development.

*Credit Functions*

1. Framing policy and guidelines for rural financial institutions.
2. Providing credit facilities to issuing organizations
3. Monitoring the flow of ground level rural credit.
4. Preparation of credit plans annually for all districts for identification of credit potential.

*Development Functions*

1. Help cooperative banks and Regional Rural Banks to prepare development actions plans for themselves.
2. Help Regional Rural Banks and the sponsor banks to enter into MoUs with state governments and cooperative banks to improve the affairs of the Regional Rural Banks.
3. Monitor implementation of development action plans of banks.
4. Provide financial support for the training institutes of cooperative banks, commercial banks and Regional Rural Banks.
5. Provide financial assistance to cooperative banks for building improved management information system, computerisation of operations and development of human resources.

*Supervisory Functions*

1. Undertakes inspection of Regional Rural Banks (RRBs) and Cooperative Banks (other than urban/primary cooperative banks) under the provisions of Banking Regulation Act, 1949.
2. Undertakes inspection of State Cooperative Agriculture and Rural Development Banks (SCARDBs) and apex non- credit cooperative societies on a voluntary basis.
3. Provides recommendations to Reserve Bank of India on issue of licenses to Cooperative Banks, opening of new branches by State Cooperative Banks and Regional Rural Banks (RRBs).
4. Undertakes portfolio inspections besides off-site surveillance of Cooperative Banks and Regional Rural Banks (RRBs).

# 10. Globalisation of Banking

Globalization has emerged as a prime mover in the Indian banking system. This has come about as a result of the policy of liberalization and opening up of banking and other sectors pursued after 1991 in India. Foreign banks that wish to set up their offices/branches in India have been granted licenses by RBI on liberal and on reciprocal basis. Similarly, Indian banks are also opening their offices/branches abroad, particularly in countries whose banks have opened offices in India.

## Technological Development

The Banking Laws (Amendment) Bill that was passed by the Parliament in 2012 allowed the Reserve Bank of India (RBI) to make final guidelines on issuing new bank licenses. Moreover, the role of the Indian Government in expanding the banking sector is noteworthy. It is expected that the new guidelines issued by RBI will curb practices of impish borrowers and streamline the loan system in the country. In the coming time, India could see a rise in the number of banks in the country, a shift in the style of operation, which could also evolve by incorporating modern technology in the industry. Another emerging trend witnessed by the banking sector is the use of social media platform like Facebook to attract customers. (In September 2013 ICICI bank launched a Facebook bill payment and fund transfer service called 'Pockets' for customer convenience).

According to a report by Zinnov, a Globalization and Market Expansion firm, 'IT adoption in BSFI sector in India', the Information Technology Industry spend in BFSI vertical is expected to reach USD 3.5 billion by Financial Year 2014. The study also highlighted 'the growing maturity of Indian BFSI organizations in IT adoption, as technology is seen as a driver of business value. Technology firms have great potential to explore in the BFSI sector, which contributes to eight per cent of India's Gross Domestic Product.'

With the advancement of technology and the birth of competition, banks are in the race of becoming the best in the country. The advancement in the technology has helped the banks to reduce the workload. There are so many activities, which are taken over by machines. The bankshave different types of activities, which are taken over by machines are as follows:

## Online Banking

Online banking (or Internet banking) is a term used for performing transactions, payments etc. over the Internet through a bank, credit union or building society's secure website. This allows customers to do their banking outside of bank hours and from anywhere where Internet access is available.

**Features of online banking**: Online banking usually offers such features as:

- Bank statements.
- Electronic bill payment
- Funds transfer.
- Loan applications and transactions, such as repayments
- Account aggregation

## Automatic Teller Machine

Automatic Teller Machine is the most popular devise in India, which enables the customers to withdraw their money 24 hours a day 7 days a week. It is a device that allows customer who has an ATM card to perform routine banking transactions without interacting with a human teller. In addition to cash withdrawal, ATMs can be used for payment of utility bills, funds transfer v between accounts, deposit of cheques and cash into accounts, balance enquiry etc.

## Tele Banking

Tele Banking facilitates the customer to do entire non-cash related banking on telephone. Under this devise Automatic Voice Recorder is used for simpler queries and transactions. For v complicated queries and transactions, manned phone terminals are used.

## Electronic Clearing Service (ECS)

ECS is an electronic mode of funds transfer from one bank account to another. Electronic Clearing Service is a retail payment system that can be used to make bulk payments/receipts of a similar nature especially where each individual payment is of a repetitive nature and of relatively smaller amount. This facility is meant for companies and government departments to make/receive large volumes of payments rather than for funds transfers by individuals. It can be used by institutions for making payments such as distribution of dividend interest, salary, pension, among others. It can also be used to pay bills and other charges such as telephone, electricity, water. ECS can be used for both credit and debit purposes.

## Electronic Funds Transfer (EFT)

Electronic Funds Transfer (EFT) is a system whereby anyone who wants to make payment to another person/company etc. can approach his bank and make cash payment or give instructions/authorization to transfer funds directly from his own account to the bank account of the receiver/beneficiary. Electronic Funds Transfer (EFT) is a system of transferring money from one bank account directly to another without any paper money changing hands. Complete details such as the receiver's name, bank account number, account type (savings or current account), bank name, city, branch name etc. should be furnished to the bank at the time of requesting for such transfers so that the amount reaches the beneficiaries' account correctly and faster. v RBI is the service provider of EFT. It is used for both credit transfers, such as payroll payments, and for debit transfers, such as mortgage payments. The growing popularity of EFT for online bill payment is paving the way for a paperless universe where checks, stamps, envelopes, and paper bills are obsolete.

*Benefits of EFT*

- Reduced administrative costs
- Increased efficiency
- Simplified bookkeeping
- Greater security.

## Real Time Gross Settlement

Real Time Gross Settlement system, introduced in India since March 2004, is a system through which electronics instructions can be given by banks to transfer funds from their account to the account of another bank. The RTGS system is maintained and operated by the RBI and provides a means of efficient and faster funds transfer among banks facilitating their financial operations. RTGS is a large value funds transfer system. As the name suggests, funds transfer between banks takes place on a 'Real Time' basis. Transfer of money takes place from one bank to another on a "real time" and on "gross basis". Therefore, money can reach the beneficiary instantaneously and the beneficiary's bank has the v responsibility to credit the beneficiary's account within two hours. Money can be transferred only to those branches in which RTGS is enable.

## Point of Sale Terminal

Point of Sale Terminal is a type of electronic-transaction terminal with computer terminal that is linked online to the computerized customer information files in a bank and magnetically encoded plastic transaction card that identifies the customer to the computer. This typically includes a computer, a cash register and other equipment or software used to sell goods or services. During a transaction, the customer's account is debited and the retailer's account is credited by the computer for the amount of purchase many activities, which are taken over by machines. The banks also transmit sales data to be posted to customer accounts. It is an electronic payment system involving electronic fund transfers based on the use of payment cards, such as debit or credit, at payment terminals located at point of sale.

## Satellite Banking

Satellite banking is an upcoming technological innovation in the Indian banking industry. Satellite banking refers to a way of organizing a bank's branch network so that it is clustered around larger branches.It is expected to help in solving the problem of weak terrestrial communication links in many parts of the country. The use of satellites for establishing connectivity between branches will help banks to reach rural and hilly areas in a better way, and offer better facilities, particularly in relation to electronic funds transfers.

## Phone Banking

**Mobile phone banking** is the use of a smartphone or other cellular device to accomplish tasks such as checking account balances, transferring funds between accounts, bill payment and finding an ATM while away from a computer.Phone and mobile banking are a fairly recent phenomenon for the Indian banking industry.

**Telephone banking** is a service provided by a bank or other financial institution, that enables customers to perform a range of financial transactions over the telephone, without the need to visit a bank branch or automated teller machine. Phone banking channels function through an Interactive Voice Response System (IVRS) or tele-banking executives of the banks. Telephone banking times are usually longer than branch opening times, and some financial institutions offer the service on a 24-hour basis. Most financial institutions have restrictions on which accounts may be accessed through telephone banking, as well as a limit on the amount that can be transacted.

*Benefits of Phone Banking*

- Account details.
- Account balance.
- Status of cheques.
- Transaction details.
- Request for registration and regeneration of email account statements.
- Register for mobile alerts
- Request for Cash Management Services MIS reports.
- Product offerings amongst others.
- Stop payment request.
- Cheque book request.

# BANCASSURANCE

Bancassurance is a French term referring to the selling of insurance through a bank's established distribution channels.  The usage of the word picked up as banks and insurance companies merged and banks sought to provide insurance, especially in markets that have been liberalised recently. Bancassurance is the term used to describe the sale of insurance products in a bank. The word is a combination of "banque or bank" and "assurance" signifying that both banking and insurance is provided by the same corporate entity. It is a controversial idea, and many feel it gives banks too great a control over the financial industry. Banks gives peace of mind with Bancassurance. One receive coverage and save money at the same time. The right option can be choose which benefits the user at most.

Bancassurance simply means selling of insurance products by banks. In this arrangement, insurance companies and banks undergo a tie-up, thereby allowing banks to sell the insurance products to its customers. By selling insurance policies bank earns a revenue stream apart from interest. It is called as fee-based income. This income is purely risk free for the bank since the bank simply plays the role of an intermediary for sourcing business to the insurance company. Insurers see it as a tool to increase penetration and market share and bankers use it to augment their fee income and to smoothen the volatility of interest income. Bancassurance is a package of banking and insurance service at one roof. The introduction of Bancassurance has broadened the scope of retail banking.

## Benefits of Bancassurance

It helps both the banks and Insurance Companies as follows:

- It encourages customers of banks to purchase insurance policies and further helps in building better relationship with the bank.
- The people who are unaware of and/or are not in reach of insurance policies can be benefitted through widely distributed banking networks and better marketing channels of banks.
- Increase in number of providers means increase in competition and hence people can expect better premium rates and better services from bancassurance as compared to traditional insurance companies.
- This is a referral business in which the banks tend to leverage the existing clientele.
- Insurance companies get the benefit because the company can have distribution relationships with multiple insurers.

## Demerits of Bancassurance

- Data management of an individual customer's identity and contact details may result in the insurance company utilizing the details to market their products, thus compromising on data security.
- There is a possibility of conflict of interest between the other products of bank and insurance policies (like money back policy). This could confuse the customer regarding where he has to invest.
- Better approach and services provided by banks to customer is a hope rather than a fact. This is because many banks in India are known for their bad customer service and this fact turns worse when the companies are responsible to sell insurance products. Work nature to market insurance products require submissive attitude, which is a point that has to be worked on by many banks in India.

## Core Banking Solutions

Core banking (stand for "centralized online real-time exchange") is a banking services provided by a group of networked bank branches. Core Banking Solution (CBS) is networking of branches, which enables Customers to operate their accounts, and avail banking services from any branch of the Bank on CBS network, regardless of where he maintains his account. This word is more often used by bankers and now-a-days postal officials are also using this system. CBS is an acronym of Core Banking Solutions. It stands for "Centralised On-line Real–time Exchange.

The customer is no more the customer of a Branch. He becomes the Bank's Customer. Another interesting fact regarding CBS is that all CBS branches are inter-connected with each other. Therefore, Customers of CBS branches can avail various banking facilities from any other CBS branch located anywhere in the world.This word is more often used by bankers and now-a-days postal officials are also using it. Here customers may access their bank account and perform basic transactions from any of the member branch offices. Larger businesses are managed via the Corporate banking division of the institution.

### Elements of Core Banking Include

- To make enquiries about the balance or debit or credit entries in the account.
- To obtain cash payment out of his account by tendering a cheque.
- To deposit a cheque for credit into his account.
- To deposit cash into the account.
- To deposit cheques or cash into account of some other person who has account in a CBS branch.
- To get statement of account.
- To transfer funds from his account to some other account his own or of third party, provided both accounts are in CBS branches.
- To obtain Demand Drafts or Banker's Cheques from any branch on CBS-amount shall be online debited to his account.
- Customers can continue to use ATMs and other Delivery Channels, which are also interfaced with CBS platform.

### Benefits to the Customers

- A CBS branch is like a Sales & Service Delivery Center. Back office processes/activities are handled through technology at some other site, called Data Center. Branch, therefore, has more time for serving customers. This improves the quality and efficiency of the services rendered and the customer is directly benefited by way of satisfying and happy banking experience.
- Since a CBS branch is essentially designed to focus on customer-interface and customer service, the special layout and ambience of the branch is made toprovide a convenient and delightful banking experience. The Customer Service Representatives/ Executives at the branch are specially trained to understand, facilitate and deliver banking services efficiently and effectively.

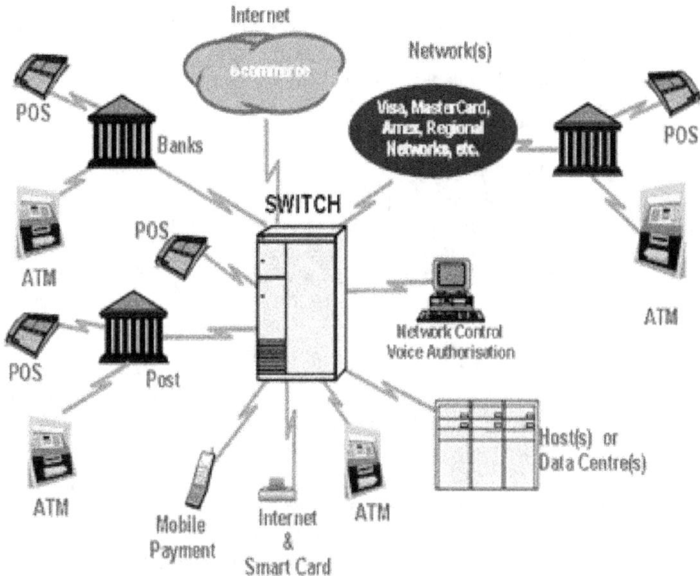


## Financial Electronic Data Interchange

FEDI combines Electronic Funds Transfer (EFT) with Electronic Data Interchange (EDI) capabilities to electronically transmit payment and remittance data to the organization. It facilitates computer to-computer exchange of electronic documents (such as purchase orders, advance shipment notices and without human intervention or human readable (paper or electronic documents). EDI is a low cost alternative to the traditional paper check method of payment. EDI electronically transfers funds from the Commonwealth's bank account to the organization's designated bank account. These electronic payments are processed through the Automated Clearing House (ACH) network. The EDI process allows our trading partners to have access to the funds on the due date.

## International Banking

Indian banks have extended their activities beyond the national boundaries. The extension may take place in the form of borrowings as well as lending and it may take place through official or private or commercial channel. In the process of internationalization, the domestic financial institutions participate in foreign financial markets and the foreign institutions participate in domestic market to a significant extent.

### International Lending

- **Syndicated Loans**: Large loans that enable borrowers to obtain large amounts of funds and lenders can diversify their credit risk. Lead bank can earn fee income for management services.
- **Letters of Credit**: Import letters of credit are issued by a bank in favor of a firm in most cases.

## Risk Management

The financial sector in various economies like that of India are undergoing a monumental change factoring into account world events such as the ongoing Banking Crisis across the globe. Risk management in Indian banks is a relatively newer practice, but has already shown to increase efficiency in governing of these banks as such procedures tend to increase the corporate governance of a financial institution.

## CRMS and ANY Branch Banking

Customer relationship management (CRM) is a system for managing a company's interactions with current and future customers. It often involves using technology to organize, automate and synchronize sales, marketing, customer service and technical. Any branch banking all the branches are inter-connected and are capable of providing online, real-time transactions to its customers. Customers can Deposit/Withdraw freely without any tariff charge.

## INFINET

The Indian Financial Network (INFINET) is the communication backbone for the Indian Banking and Financial sector. All Banks, Public Sector, Private Sector, Foreign, Cooperative etc., and premier Financial Institutions in the country are eligible to become members of the INFINET.

The INFINET is a Closed User Group (CUG) Network and uses a blend of communication technologies such as VSATs and Terrestrial Leased Lines. The network consists of over 700 VSATs located in 127 cities of the country and utilizes one full transponder on INSAT 3B. The Hub of the VSAT network is situated at the Institute for Development and Research in Banking Technology (IDRBT), Hyderabad, and consists of an 11-meter antenna and other satellite earth station equipments. This Hub is manned round the clock. Inaugurated on June 19, 1999, various inter-bank and intrabank applications ranging from Simple Messaging, MIS, EFT, ECS, Electronic Debit, Online Processing and Trading in Government Securities, Centralised Funds querying for Banks and Financial Institutions, Anywhere/Anytime Banking, and Inter-Branch Reconciliation are being implemented using the INFINET.

The INFINET is primarily a TCP/IP based network. A detailed IP addressing scheme has been devised by IDRBT for all CUG members, which has to be strictly followed by all CUG members while interacting via the INFINET communication backbone. Every CUG member has to sign a Memorandum of Understanding with IDRBT for availing the services. The INFINET is being expanded using leased line technology wherein 21 cities are being connected by a judicious mix of bandwidth and enough redundancy and back-up leased line links. CUG members will be allowed gateways to this leased line based network at each of these 21 cities. The leased line segment of the INFINET will be seamlessly integrated with the VSAT portion of the INFINET.

INFINET can be used for both intra and interbank applications. Banks can develop and port intra bank applications on their own. Interbank applications are being developed together by the Reserve Bank of India, IDRBT and member banks. Applications such as Real Time Gross Settlement, Central Funds Management System, Security Settlement System, Electronic Clearing System and Electronic Funds Transfer, being developed by the RBI will be ported on the INFINET and in a true sense, the INFINET will become the backbone for the National Payment Systems. These applications will use the SFMS platform. Some of the applications, which the CUG members are using on the network are Any Branch Banking (Multi Branch Banking), Fast Collection of Cheques, Cash Management Products, ATM Network, Interbank reconciliation, Corporate E-mails etc.

## SWIFT

SWIFT stands for Society for Worldwide Interbank Financial Telecommunication (SWIFT). SWIFT is a cooperative society under Belgian law owned by its member financial institutions with offices around the world. SWIFT headquarters, designed by Ricardo Bofill Taller de Arquitectura are in La Hulpe, Belgium, near Brussels. It's automated payment system used to transfer funds between different countries, Global communication network that facilitates 24-hour secure international exchange of payment instructions between banks, centralbanks,multinational corporations, and major securities firms.

It provides a network that enables financial institutions worldwide to send and receive information about financial transactions in a secure, standardized and reliable environment. A member owned cooperative organized in 1977 under Belgium law, it now includes over 6,500 participating members from more than180 countries which together process in excess of a billion messages every year. SWIFT transports financial messages in a highly secure way but does not hold accounts for its members and does not perform any form of clearing or settlement.

## Universal Banking

Universal banking is a system of banking where banks undertake a blanket of financial services like investment banking, commercial banking, development banking, insurance and other financial services including functions of merchant banking, mutual funds, factoring, housing finance, insurance etc. In simple words, Universal Banking means that Financial Institutions (FIs) and Banks are allowed to undertake all kinds of activity of banking, financing and related businesses.

As per the World Bank, the definition of the Universal Bank is as follows: In Universal banking, the large banks operate extensive network of branches, provide many different services, hold several claims on firms (including equity and debt) and participate directly in the Corporate Governance of firms that rely on the banks for funding or as insurance underwriters. Therefore Universal bank is a Financial Supermarket which provides all financial products under one roof.

Apart from savings and loans, the Universal banks provides services such as investing in securities, credit cards, project finance, remittances, payment systems, project counselling, merchant banking, forex operations, insurance and so on. In a nutshell, a Universal Banking is a superstore for financial products under one roof. Corporate can get loans and avail of other handy services, while can deposit and borrow. It includes not only services related to savings and loans but also investments.

Universal Banking is usually undertaken by large banks who can manage the cost of such widespread operations. The concept was culmination of reports submitted by Narasimham Committee and S.H. Khan Committee which had suggested to consolidate the financial industry of India via medium of merging financial activities carried by different types of financial institutions.

**Universal Banking in India:** The second Narasimham committee of 1998 gave an introductory remark on the concept of the Universal banking, as a different concept than the Narrow Banking. Narsimham Committee II suggested that Development Financial Institutions (DFIs) should convert ultimately into either commercial banks or non-bank finance companies. However, the concept of Universal Banking conceptualized in India after the RH Khan Committee recommended it as a different concept. The Khan Working Group held the view that DFIs (Development Finance Institutions) should be allowed to become banks at the earliest.

## *Advantages of Universal Banking*

The **benefits** or advantages of universal banking are:

**Investors' Trust:** Universal banks hold stakes (equity shares) of many companies. These companies can easily get other investors to invest in their business. This is because other investors have full confidence and faith in the Universal banks. The investors knows that the Universal banks will closely watch all the activities of the companies in which the investor hold a stake.

1. **Economics of Scale:** Universal banking results in economic efficiency. That is, it results in lower costs, higher output and better products and services. In India, RBI is in favour of universal banking because it results in economies of scale.
2. **Resource Utilisation:** Universal banks use their client's resources as per the client's ability to take a risk. If the client has a high risk taking capacity then the universal bank will advise him to make risky investments and not safe investments. Similarly, clients with a low risk taking capacity are advised to make safe investments. Today, universal banks invest their client's money in different types of Mutual funds and also directly into the share market. Thebank also do equity research. So, the client can also manage their client's portfolios (different investments) profitably.
3. **Profitable Diversification:** Universal banks diversify their activities. So, the bank can use the same financial experts to provide different financial services. This saves cost for the universal bank. Even the day-to-day expenses will be saved because all financial services are provided under one roof, i.e. in the same office.
4. **Easy Marketing:** The universal banks can easily market (sell) all their financial products and services through their many branches. The bank can ask their existing clients to buy their other products and services. This requires less marketing efforts because of their well-established brand name. For e.g. ICICI may ask their existing bank account holders in all their branches, to take house loans, insurance, to buy their Mutual funds, etc. This is done very easily because thebankuse one brand name (ICICI) for all their financial products and services.
5. **One-stop Shopping:** Universal banking offers all financial products and services under one roof. One-stop shopping saves a lot of time and transaction costs. It also increases the speed or flow of work. So, one-stop shopping gives benefits to both banks and their clients.

## *Disadvantages of Universal Banking*

The limitations or disadvantages of universal banking are:

1. **Different Rules and Regulations:** Universal banking offers all financial products and services under one roof. However, all these products and services have to follow different rules and regulations. This creates many problems. For e.g. Mutual Funds, Insurance, Home Loans, etc. have to follow different sets of rules and regulations, but the rules are provided by the same bank.

2. **Effect of failure on Banking System**: Universal banking is done by very large banks. If these huge banks fail, then it will have a very big and bad effect on the banking system and the confidence of the public. For e.g. Recently, Lehman Brothers a very large universal bank failed. It had very bad effects in the USA, Europe and even in India.
3. **Monopoly**: Universal banks are very large. So, the bank can easily get monopoly power in the market. This will have many harmful effects on the other banks and the public. This is also harmful to economic development of the country.
4. **Conflict of Interest**: Combining commercial and investment banking can result in conflict of interest. That is, Commercial banking versus Investment banking. Some banks may give more importance to one type of banking and give less importance to the other type of banking. However, this does not make commercial senses.

## Corporate Banking

Corporate banking is defined as custom-tailored financing and banking services or corporations. Corporate banking is typically offered by commercial banks, and entails all the services that can be extended on a financial level to corporate entities to ease day-to-day operations.

### *Features of Corporate Banking*

Corporate Bankingis financial operations that involve large-scale companies, government organizations and other significant institutions. The operations are conducted by both retail and investment banks, and many of those banks are large national or international entities. Many of those operations are general banking activities such as deposit taking, lending and e-banking. Others, however, are more specifically tailored to their corporate clients' needs. And while the specifics of those corporate bank operations vary with each bank, but all have certain common features.

1. **International Transactions:** Banks can facilitate foreign exchange transactions and provide trade financing. The banks can also work to protect their customers by mitigating the impact of currency and price fluctuations.
2. **Investment Banking:** Bad credit card loans will generally cost borrowers more in interest than other types of financing available. If keeping costs down as much as possible is the plan, seeking out reasonably priced vehicles is not a bad idea. This, however, does not mean that new cars need to be removed from the picture entirely. Sometimes purchase incentives make new cars the wiser and even "cheaper" purchase on a monthly basis than used.
3. **Project Financing:** Banks offer loans for large-scale projects, particularly infrastructure projects. Those loans are repaid based on the revenue the project winds up generating. If the project is deemed particularly risky, a group of banks can agree to lend the client portions of the required loan. That way, if the risk doesn't pay off, the fallout is reduced for every bank involved.
4. **Insurance:** Banks offer insurance to their large-scale clients. The insurance can cover corporate activities, as well as staff and management.
5. **Advisory Services:** Banks offer financial advice for an assortment of corporate and financial activities. That includes:
   - Mergers and acquisitions
   - Asset management
   - Taxation issues, such as using tax havens.

6. **Corporate Brokerage Services:** Banks offer corporate brokerage services, negotiating financial transactions, particularly mergers and acquisitions. This can include working with clients that want to either:
   - sell off all or part of their businesses
   - acquire businesses and parts of the businesses
   - raise the funds necessary to make the above-mentioned transactions successful
7. **Shareholding:** Banks can manage and own shares of their client companies. This is usually done to assist financially distressed companies. Buying shares can provide it with extra liquidity.
8. **Asset Custody:** Banks can protect their clients' corporate assets. This includes setting up accounts to store them, making regular audits to make sure that the bank remain intact and issuing reports that assess the assets' status on annual bases.

## Difference between Corporate Banking and Commercial Banking

### Corporate Banking

Corporate banking is defined as custom-tailored financing and banking services for corporations. Corporate banking is typically offered by commercial banks, and entails all the services that can be extended on a financial level to corporate entities to ease day-to-day operations. Cash management, working capital loans and commercial mortgages are just some of the products available in this form of banking; some banks even offer financial supply chain optimization.

### Commercial Banking

Commercial banking is a provision of banking and other related services for profit. Commercial banks are incorporated companies with the main activities of accepting deposits and disbursing loans, or of exercising fiduciary rights similar to national banks. The bank also open personal and checking accounts and offer mortgages and business loans. The major differences are:

1. **Clientele:** The major difference between corporate and commercial banking is in the clientele. Corporate banking mainly deals with corporations and institutions, whereas commercial banking deals with individuals and lower-tier businesses.
2. **Service:** Commercial banking serves to provide for the normal banking needs of both corporate and non-corporate entities, while corporate banking, with its high specialization, serves to suit the welfare of a targeted few. The difference is evident by the industry specialization characteristic of corporate banking.
3. **Qualification:** A striking difference between corporate and commercial banking is in the eligibility factor. The business account for business can be quickly registered and request commercial services, but need to be of corporate strength to qualify for corporate services.
4. **Categorization:** Corporate banking is merely a banking sub-category of commercial banking. Commercial banking, on the other hand, may be divided into retail and wholesale banking.

## CRM in Banking Sector

Information technology can be helpful in supporting the search for competitive advantage. The electronic exchange of transaction documents has had a significant impact on business practices. EDI brings in many benefits to the organization such as reduced costs, faster turnaround, better customer service, and in some firms strategic advantage over their competitors. The new competitive strategies will be increasingly technologybased global initiatives that are affected by the firms' IT maturity. According to a RBI statement, in future India will have a competitive banking market as one of the most attractive market after

2009.India will see foreign banks come in, what with more freedom to come in. grow and acquire. Therefore, it is imperative that Indian banks wake up to this reality and re-focus on their core asset the Customer. A greater focus on Customer Relationship Management (CRM) is the only way the banking industry can protect its market share and boost growth.

*Factors Influencing Banking Sector*

Many banks are still following the traditional ways of marketing and only few banks are making attempts to adapt CRM. The focus of CRM helped banks to understand the customer's current needs, what the bank have done in the past, and what the banks plan to do in the future to meet their own goals. There are various factors influencing banking sector to implement CRM:

- Increasing competition
- Proliferating customer contact
- Intensifying attacks on customer information
- Rising customer expectations
- Identifying new marketing opportunities

Online customers have a special set of expectations that set them apart from traditional customers. In particular, customers expect lots of information about the company and products to be available online with minimal searching, close to immediate service, opportunities for self-service via website, and speedy shipment of products or services. Therefore, CRM principles need to be considered when doing business online. CRM is the hot talk in the banking sector. Banks are realizing that CRM is the magic bullet that helps financial institutions to build stronger and more profitable relationships.

# 11.  CREDIT CARD

## Introduction

A Credit card is a card or mechanism which enables cardholders to purchase goods, travel and dine in a hotel without making immediate payments. The holders can use the cards to get credit from banks up to 50 days free of cost. The credit card relieves the consumers from botheration of the carrying cash and ensures safety. It is a convenience of extended credit without formality. Thus credit card is a passport to, "safety, convenience, prestige and credit."

A credit card is a plastic card having a magnetic strip, issued by a bank or business authorizing the holder to buy goods or services on credit. Any card, plate or coupon book that may be used repeatedly to borrow money or buy goods and services on credit is called credit card.

A credit card allows consumers to purchase products or services without cash and to pay for them at a later date. To qualify for this type of credit, the consumer must open an account with a bank, which sponsors a card. They then receive a line of credit with a specified amount. They can use the card to make purchases from participating merchants until they reach this credit limit. Every month the sponsor provides a bill, which tallies the card activity during the previous 30 days. Depending on the terms of the card, the customer may pay interest charges on the amount that they do not pay for on a monthly basis. Also, credit cards may be sponsored by large retailers or by banks or corporations.

Credits cards are a relatively recent development. In 1977 the name Visa was adopted internationally to cover all these cards. VISA became the first credit card to be recognized worldwide. The banks and companies that sponsor credit cards profit in three ways. Primarily they make money from the interest payments charged on the unpaid balance, but they also can make money by charging an annual fee for the use of the card. The income from this fee can be substantial considering that the larger companies have tens of millions of customers. In addition, the sponsors make money by charging merchants a small percentage of income for the service of the card. This arrangement is acceptable to the merchants because they can let their customers pay by credit card instead of requiring cash. The merchant makes arrangements to participate in a credit card program with a merchant bank, which in turn works with a card-issuing bank. The merchant bank determines what percentage of the total purchase value has to be paid by the merchant to the card-issuing bank. The amount varies depending on the volume and type of business. A percentage of that amount is kept by the merchant bank as a transaction-processing fee. Furthermore, sponsors may generate income by leasing credit card verification equipment to merchants.  Finally, sponsors may profit by charging service fees for late payments.

## Anatomy of a Credit Card

The long string of numbers, the magnetic stripe, the signature strip, the bank logo-each plays a role in making credit transactions work.

Credit cards are designed with complex security features to prevent the possibility of fraud. These features involve the card's account number, its signature panel, and its magnetic stripe. The card's unique account number is the key piece of information needed to conduct a financial transaction and must be carefully protected. To prevent someone from using a wrong account number, or from making up a phony number, companies rely on the laws of statistics for protection. By using long account numbers they make it unlikely that a number can be faked.

For example, the Visa card has 13 digits, American Express has 15, Diners Club 14, and MasterCard has 20. Mathematically, nine digits would provide one billion unique account numbers (000000000, 000000001, 0000000002, and so forth up to 999999999) which would be enough for all the customers of a given company. If an incorrect account number is mistakenly entered by a store clerk, it will almost certainly not be accepted. This statistical security gives companies confidence that someone is not making up a number when conducting business over the phone. This security measure does not help if someone obtains a real number and uses it fraudulently.

Another security design feature involves the signature panel on the back of the card. The signature is intended to document the owner's handwriting so a forged signature on a receipt can be detected. To prevent criminals from erasing the back panel of a stolen card and putting on their own signature, the panel is printed with a fingerprint design that is difficult to duplicate and that will come off when the original signature is erased. If the signature is erased, this design will disappear too leaving a white spot, which instantly indicates the card has been tampered with. Some card manufacturers imprint the word VOID beneath this panel, which is revealed upon erasure.

The magnetic stripe on the back of the card is a third security feature. The stripe is an area coated with particles of iron oxide that can be encoded with binary information, which identifies the card as authentic. It is difficult to determine exactly what information is coded on the strip because for security reasons companies do not wish to discuss this. However, it is likely that the card's expiration date is one fact recorded on the strip because automatic teller machines (ATMs) will retain cards that have expired. It is unlikely that information like credit limit, address, phone number, employer, is recorded on the stripe because banks do not reissue cards when this type of information changes. Finally, some cards feature special features that make them hard to duplicate, such as complicated holograms.

*Bank Logo*

This is the logo of the bank that actually issued the card. The entity that is lending money, not the one that processes payments. Sometimes, as with American Express or Discover, they're the same, so there is only one logo.

*Computer Chip*

The computer chip is being phased in for credit cards in the United States to boost security. The chips generate a unique code for every transaction, while magnetic stripes have unchanging information that can be stolen and reused. Chip cards may be used in conjunction with a PIN or signature.

*A Hologram*

A hologram is an optional three-dimensional image embedded into a two-dimensional surface serves to distinguish real cards from counterfeits.

*First Six Digits*

The first six digits tell merchants who issued the card. The very first number is the "Major Industry Identifier." For example, a "1" denotes an airline. All Visa cards, for example, start with a 4, Master Cards a 5 and Discover cards a 6.

The maximum length of a credit card number is 19 digits, but most cards have 16. The final digit is a "checksum" number that, using the "Luhn formula," allows the validity of a card's number series to be instantly verified, preventing casual theft and data entry errors. The first and last name of the cardholder or the organization associated with the account.

Online transactions often require the name on the card exactly match the cardholder name. The "valid thru" or expiration date is the last month and year the credit card can be used. Sometimes a day of the month, normally first or last, is included.

## Materials

Cards are made of several layers of plastic laminated together. The core is commonly made from a plastic resin known as polyvinyl chloride acetate. This resin is mixed with pacifying materials, dyes, and plasticizers to give it the proper appearance and consistency. This core material is laminated with thin layers of clear plastic materials. These laminates will adhere to the core when applied with pressure and heat.

A variety of inks or dyes are also used for printing credit cards. These are available in a variety of colors and are designed for use on plastic substrates. Some manufacturers use special magnetic inks to print the magnetic stripe on the back of the card. The inks are made by dispersing metal oxide particles in the appropriate solvents. Additional special printing processes are involved for cards, like VISA, which feature holograms.

## Quality Control

Key quality issues are associated with the compounding of plastic and color matching of the inks. The American National Standards Institute has a standard for plastic raw materials. As with any compounding procedure, ingredients must be properly weighed and mixed and blended under the appropriate temperature and sheer conditions. Similarly, the molding process must be monitored to avoid defects, which could cause the cards to crack or break. The final quality check is to make sure the correct numbers are stamped on the cards during the embossing process.

## Future Outlook

Future credit card manufacturing processes are likely to evolve in three key areas. First, continued improvements in plastic chemistry and molding technology are likely to allow cards to be made increasingly cheaper and easier. Second, breakthroughs in digital technology are likely to improve the way credit cards are kept secure with advanced magnetic coding. One recent advance is the use of a new generation of magnetic stripes which are harder to duplicate. This improvement combats the trend toward duplicating card information and copying it to phony cards. Perhaps even more importantly, new generations of credit cards will carry integrated computer chips, containing a variety of useful information. For instance, these future cards will be able to operate a frequent flyer program on the same card as a debit or credit account. Other services will allow users to participate in frequency or loyalty programs with merchants, including storing hotel reservation preferences. Financial institutions may develop partnerships with local mass transit systems so public transit could be paid for with these "smart" cards in various cities throughout the world. Third, marketing initiatives resulting from these advances in card technology are likely to make credit cards even more pervasive in society.

## Operations of Credit Cards

A credit card is a plastic payment card which is used to borrow money to pay for goods and services. Unlike a debit card, where money is taken directly from current account, anything paid for using a credit card will be added onto card's balance. Ideally, one should pay off this balance every month when the bill comes through but if can't, the card provider will still insist to repay a stated minimum.

## Definitions

### i. *Annual Fee*

A fee some credit card companies charge for having the card and its benefits.

### ii. *Annual Interest Rate*

When not paid off purchases in full by the payment date on credit card bill and to carry a balance forward from the previous month. The annual interest rate is the rate of interest charged on the balance that carried forward.

### iii. *Account Balance*

The total account debt as of the statement date taking into account the previous balance:

- Minus any payments you had made since the previous statement.
- Plus new purchases and cash advances.
- Plus interest charges and other fees.

### iv. *Credit Limit*

The credit limit is the amount of credit assigned to the account. The credit limit determined is based on the previous credit behaviour and a number of other factors such as:

- Monthly income
- Current debt (credit cards, student loan, line of credit, etc.)
- Home ownership
- Length of time at current residence
- Length of time at current employer
- Number of times the holder have obtained credit
- How much credit needed
- Previous debt repayment history.

### v. *Grace Period*

The number of days between the statement date and the date to pay before charging interest, provided that paid off full balance in the previous month.

### vi. *Minimum Payment*

The smallest amount required to pay by the payment due date to ensure account remains in good standing. This is indicated on statement as the "Current month's minimum payment".

### vii. *Over Limit Fee*

A fee charged for exceeding your credit limit. Exceeding the limit may damage credit record since it's considered a breach of the credit agreement.

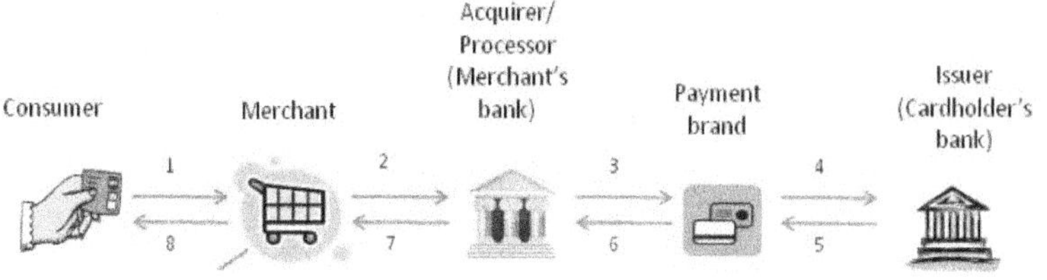

## Types of Credit Cards

### Based on Banking Validity

#### i. *Proprietary Card*

Cards that are issued by the banks themselves without any tie-up, are called proprietary cards. A bank issues such cards under its own brand. Examples include SBI Card, Can Card of Canara Bank, Citi card.

#### ii. *Master Card*

This is a type of credit card issued under the umbrella of MasterCard International. The issuing bank has to obtain a franchise from the MasterCard Corporation of the USA. The franchised cards will be honoured in the MasterCard network.

#### iii. *VISA Card*

This type of credit card can be issued by any bank having tie-up with VISA International Corporation, USA. The banks that issue such cards are said to have a franchise of VISA International. The advantage of a VISA franchise is that one can avail the facility of the VISA network for transactions.

#### iv. *Domestic tie-up Card*

These cards are issued by a bank having a tie-up with domestic card brands such as CanCard and Indcard are called 'Domestic cards'.

### Based on Geographical Validity

#### i. *Domestic Card*

Cards that are valid only in India and Nepal are called 'domestic cards'. They are issued by most of the banks in India all transactions will be in rupees.

#### ii. *International and Global Card*

Credit cards with international validity are called 'international cards'. They are issued to people who travel abroad frequently. They are honoured in every part of the world except India and Nepal. The cardholder can make purchases in foreign currencies subject to RBI sanction and FERA rules and regulations.

### Based on the Issuer Category

#### i. *Individual Card*

These are the non-corporate credit cards that are issued to individuals. Generally, all brands of credit cards are issued to individuals.

#### ii. *Corporate Card*

They are credit cards issued to corporate and business firms. The executives and top officials of the firms use them. They bear the names of the firms, and the bills are paid by the firms

## Based on Mode of Credit Recovery

### i.    Revolving Card

This type of credit card is based on the revolving credit principle. A credit limit is fixed on the amount of money one can spend on the card for a particular period. The cardholder has to pay a minimum percentage of the outstanding credit which may vary from 5 to 10 percent at the end of a particular period. Interest varying from 30 to 36 percent per annum is charged on the outstanding amount.

### ii.    Charge Card

A charge card is not a credit instrument, it is a convenient mode of making payment. This facility gives a consolidated for a specific periods and bills are payable in full on presentation. There is neither interest liability nor no per-set spending limits.

## Based on Status of Card

### i.    Standard Card

Credit cards that are regularly issued by all card-issuing banks are called 'standard cards'. With these cards, it is possible for a cardholder to make purchases without having to pay cash immediately. They however, offer only limited privileges to cardholders. Some banks issue standard cards under the Brand name "Classic" cards, which are generally issued to salaried people.

### ii.    Business Card

Business cards also known as 'Executive cards', are issued to small partnership firms, solicitors, firms of chartered accountants, tax consultants and others, for use by executives on their business trips. They enjoy higher credit limits and more privileges than the standard cards.

### iii.    Gold Card

The gold card offers high value credit for elite. It offers many additional benefits and facilities such as higher credit limits, more cash advance limits that are not available with the standard or the executive cards.

## Based on Innovative Card

In addition, credit cards which have evolved into a variety of innovative cards over the years are also issued by banks.

### i.    ATM Card

ATM cards allow customers to access their accounts at any time-24 hours a day, every day of the year, through Automated Teller Machines. Customers can withdraw cash, transfer funds, find out their account balance and perform other banking and financial transactions with the help of ATMs.

### ii.    Debit Card

A debit card, like an ATM card, directly accesses a customer's account. It is a hybrid of ATM and credit card. The card directly debits a designated savings bank account. Whereas in the case of credit cards, a grace credit period of 20 to 50 days for making the payment is available, no such credit period is allowed under debit cards. These cards can be used either at merchant locations who have this facility to buy goods and services or at ATMs. Presently, ATM-Cum Debit cards issued by Indian banks are in use.

*iii.    Prepaid Card*

Prepaid cards are also known as 'Stored Value Cards'. These cards are with stored value paid in advance by the holder. The card issuer and the service provider are identical. They are also called Limited Purpose Prepaid Cards which can be used for a limited number of well-defined purposes. Its use is often restricted to a number of identified points of sales within a specified location.

*iv.    Private Label Card*

These cards are uniquely tied to the retailer issuing the card and can be used only in that retailer's stores. A bank, on the basis of a contractual agreement with the retailer extends credit under this type of card.

*v.    Affinity Group Card*

These are credit cards designed for a collection of individuals with some form of common interest or relationship, such as professional, alumni, retired persons' organizations, sports teams, schools, or service organizations. This credit card carries the logo of the affiliated organization on the card design and brings special benefits and discounts on products from that company. In case the affiliated company is a charity or non-profit organization, a part of the credit card expenses go into the affiliate organization's account.

*vi.    Smart Card*

A smart card is a credit card sized plastic card with an embedded computer chip. The chip allows the card to carry a much greater amount of information than a magnetic strip card. The telecom industry, was perhaps the pioneer in smart cards, the most prominent being Subscriber Identity Module (SIM) cards in the GMS digital cellular network. Using special terminals designated to interact with the embedded chip, the card can perform special functions. This is essentially a prepaid card.

*vii.    Chip Card*

A chip card is a plastic card with an embedded integrated circuit or as microchip as opposed to magnetic strips on a conventional card. The chip can be used on existing debit and credit cards as well as on emerging products like stored value cards. Inserting the card in a pin-pad effects the transaction, and the value on it reduces accordingly. It is re-loadable and disposable. The idea is to do away with the trouble of carrying cash. The chip card also scores over the magnetic card, in that it can retain 50 to 60 of the latest transactions, which can be produced on demand. It is also considered more durable and secure since the cardholder alone can access it through a Personal Identification Number (PIN).

*viii.    Co-branded Card*

The Times Card, a co-branded credit card, is the first of its kind, from a publishing house in the Asian subcontinent. This is a co-branded credit card of Times of India Group and Citibank MasterCard. The co-branding concept caught the credit card industry the world over during the last five years.

## Other types of Credit Card

*i.    Special Purpose Card*

The eighties saw the development of special purpose cards. A host of special purpose cards were issued by departmental stores, airlines, oil companies. For instance, the International Bank of Asia in Hong Kong launched the first 'women only' card, 'My card' in the year 1988.

A highly encouraging membership and increasing potential of such special purpose cards are called "Lady's card" in Malaysia. In 1990, the Green card was launched in the U.K and Europe to promote contributions towards the protection of the environment. HDFC issued 'My City' credit cards used in particular city with special discount offer for oil and petrol and also an offer for cash back. AXIS Bank also offers special purpose credit cards like Gift card, Travel currency card and Remittance card.

## ii.    Add-on Card

An add-on card is more of an additional Credit card that the customer can apply in the name of their family members (father, mother, sister, brother, spouse, children), within the overall credit limit. Family members applying for Add-on cards have to be 18 years and above. All the payments for the services made from Add-on card(s) is done by the original cardholders. Most banks allow for at least two Add-on cards.

## iii.    Photo Card

If a card comes with the imprinted photo, then it is a Photo card. This type of card is considered safer as it is easier to identify the credit card user. It also serves as more identity card.

## iv.    Power Card

It is a comprehensive credit card product that enables banks and financial industry to enter into issuing and acquiring business of Credit Cards. The basic advantage of this efficient tool is to improve productivity and control the risks involved in day-to-day activities of any financial institutions in credit cards. The product is 24×7, multi language, multi currency, multi-bank and multi country.

## v.    Regular Credit Card

This is the most basic type of credit card. It has a low credit limit and the most basic status among various credit cards. Credit card companies can club various other reward programs like travel rewards, cash back offers to enhance its value and appeal to customers.

## vi.    Silver Credit Card

Silver credit cards have higher eligibility criteria than regular credit cards. They bring more benefits to the customers, and have higher credit limits than regular credit cards.

## vii.    Gold Credit Card

Gold credit cards have a higher status and credit limits than silver credit cards. Needless to say these types of credit cards have higher income requirements as their eligibility criteria. In addition to the regular benefits, banks extend special privileges to their gold credit card holders.

## viii.    Platinum or Titanium Credit Card

These types of credit cards bring more benefits to credit card holders than regular, silver or gold card. These credit cards generally have platinum or titanium hue and are issued to a select class of clients who have excellent financial background and good income levels. Platinum credit cards have personal concierge services, in addition to exclusive platinum benefits.

## ix.    Signature Credit Card

A league of its own, the Signature Credit Cards usually have no pre-set spending limits, personal concierge service, signature travel, and lounge and membership benefits. Offered to a very elite group these credit cards, requires an excellent financial status. On June 9, 2007 ICICI bank introduced the Visa Signature Card and became the first credit card issuer in India to launch a premium credit card. This has a joining fee of Rs.25,000/- and an annual fee of Rs.2,500/-. The exclusivity of this signature card is exemplified by the statement.

### x.    *Credit Cards by Invitation Only*

The earliest of the elite, no one can apply for these cards. For example, the American Express Black Credit Card, popularly called the Centurion Card, is issued by invitation to the most exclusive and elite, to those who spend a certain minimum amount (which can run into crores of rupees).

These cards have huge annual fees and minimum spending levels. In fact, these credit cards are so exclusive, that they have an aura of mystery surrounding them and are considered status symbols.

### xi.    *Reward Card*

There are cards which offer rewards for specific kinds of purchases. For example, the Airline Reward Card offer rewards on air travel, Cash back card offer cash rewards on every card purchases, Fuel Reward Card offer rebates on petroleum and other fuel purchases from specified outlets and preferred partners. Similarly, Hotel Reward Card give rebates on hotel stay and related expenses and Health Rewards Card give benefits on medical expenses, health treatments and related activities. The rewards offered by credit card companies in alliance with various brands and stores, make them more attractive for the credit card holders.

### xii.    *Student Credit Card*

As the name implies, these credit cards are especially designed for students and help them start their credit card journey. These bring lots of rewards especially suited for students, which help them save time, money and enjoy their student life. They are a first step towards building credit history. A good credit history goes a long way in creating a relationship with banks helping to secure much needed loans and credit in the future.

### xiii.    *Special Feature Credit Card*

Credit cards can also be grouped on the basis of their features. For example, based on their introductory interest rates, credit cards can be low introductory interest credit cards, or 0 (zero) Interest credit cards. The Zero introductory interest credit cards provide interest free credit (0%) for a specified time period, which is called the introductory period. Similar is the case with credit cards that come without any annual fee what so ever and are called 'no annual fee' credit cards.

### xiv.    *Balance Transfer Credit Card*

Credit card companies provide lucrative offers with 0 per cent introductory interest or low introductory interest charges on balance transfers. This allows credit card holders to transfer the outstanding balances on their existing credit cards to a credit card with low or zero interest on balance transfers. This brings them a lot of savings in the interest rates. The balance transfer credit cards may charge a balance transfer fees for every such operation.

### xv.    *Kisan Credit Card (KCC)*

The Kisan Credit Card Scheme aims at providing need based and timely credit support to the farmers for their cultivation needs as well as non-farm activities and cost effective manner to bring about flexibility and operational freedom in credit utilization. The Kisan Card is for a period of 3 years subject to an annual review. It was launched in 1998-99 by the Government of India in consultation with the Reserve Bank of India and National Bank for Agricultural and Rural Development is a huge hit with the farmers in India. According to the RBI, presently there are about 66.56 million Kisan Credit Cards in use across India, which have been issued by various banks.

*xvi.    Secured Credit Card*

Secured credit card is a type of credit card secured by a deposit account owned by the cardholder. This deposit is held in a special savings account. The cardholder of a secured credit card is still expected to make regular payments, as with a regular card, but should they default on a payment, the card issuer has the option of recovering the cost of the purchases paid to the merchants out of the deposit. The advantage of the secured card for an individual with negative or no credit history is that most companies report regularly to the major credit bureaus. This allows for building of positive credit history.

## Comparison between Credit Card and Debit Card

|  | Credit Card | Debit Card |
|---|---|---|
| **About** | Credit cards are lines of credit. While using a credit card, the issuer puts money toward the transaction. This is a loan expected to pay back in full (usually within 30 days), unless to be charged interest. | When a debit card used to buy something, money is deducted from account. With a debit card, the money can only be spent. |
| **Connected To** | Not required to be connected to a checking account. | Checking or Savings Account |
| **Monthly Bills** | Yes | No |
| **Application Process** | Somewhat difficult, depending on one's credit score and other details. | Easy, with basically no barrier to receiving a debit card. |
| **Spending Limit** | The credit limit set by the credit issuer. Limits increase or stay the same over time as a borrower's creditworthiness changes. | However much is in the bank account connected to the card. |
| **Interest Charged** | If a credit card bill is not paid in full, interest is charged on outstanding balance. The interest rate is usually very high. | No interest is charged because no money is borrowed. |
| **Security** | Credit cards in the U.S. are not very secure in and of themselves because many still use dated card security technology. However, consumers are not held liable for this poor security. | A PIN makes them secure so long as no one steals the card number and PIN, and as long as the holder don't lose the card itself. If the card/info is stolen, debit cards are very insecure. |
| **Fraud Liability** | Low. Rarely held liable for fraudulent activity. If holder, holder is only held liable for a maximum of Rs.50. | High. If someone steals the card and makes purchases, that money is removed from bank account. Investigating this damage takes time. The longer delayed to report the fraud, the more likely will be held liable for own losses. |
| **Credit History** | Responsible credit card usage and payment can improve one's credit rating. Credit cards typically report account activity to at least one of the three major credit bureaus on a monthly basis. | Does not affect credit history. |
| **Overdraw Fees** | Low. Some credit card companies allow to overdraw amount over the maximum credit line with a fee. | High "overdraft" fees. Possible to overdraw amount over the account limit. |
| **PIN** | In the U.S., this is uncommon, but PINs are being phased in. | Usually |

## Credit Card Operation

The credit card operation comprises the following steps as follows:

1. **Credit purchases:** A Cardholder purchases goods/services and gives the credit card.
2. **Processing of credit card:** A Merchant establishment delivers goods after taking an authenticated credit card and noting the number and taking signatures on certain forms.
3. **Raising of bill:** The Merchant establishment raises the bill for the purchase and sends it to the credit card issuing bank for payment.
4. **Marking payment:** The issuing bank pays the amount to the merchant establishment.
5. **Bill to cardholder:** The issuing bank raises bill on the credit cardholder and sends it for payment.
6. **Card Payment:** The credit cardholder makes the payment to the issuing bank.

## Parties Involved in a Credit Card

The following important parties involved in the operation of credit cards are:

### i.     Credit Cardholders

The person named on the card. This may be customer of a bank to whom the card has been issued or any such person to whom the bank has issued a card authorized by the customer of the bank to hold and use the card. This individual is also responsible for payment of all charges made to that card. The holder of the credit card who uses to make a purchase is called the consumer.

### ii.     Card-issuing Bank

The financial institution or other organization that issued the credit card are also responsible for billing the cardholders for charges. The bank bills the consumer for repayment and bears the risk that the card is used fraudulently. The issuing bank extends a line of credit to the consumer. Liability for non-payment is then shared by the issuing bank and acquiring bank.

### iii.     Merchant Establishments

The individual or business accepting credit cards for sold products or services to the cardholders.

### iv.     Acquiring Bank

The financial institution accepts payment for the products or services on behalf of the merchant establishments.

### v.     Independent Sales Organization

Resellers (to merchants) of the services of the acquiring bank. i.e outside services providers for marketing of cards.

### vi.     Merchant Account

This could refer to the acquiring bank or the independent sales organization, but in general is the organization that the merchant deals with.

## Calculation of Finance Charge

Since there can be a significant difference in the total amount of finance charges among various cards, it is important to know how the interest rate is calculated. The credit card company will use one of three methods:

*1.  Average Daily Balance Method*

This is the most commonly used method. If credit given for payment from the day the credit card issuer receives it and the interest is calculated on the basis of the average amount owed during the previous month.

*2.  Adjusted Balance Method*

This method is the most beneficial to the consumer and produces the lowest finance charges. The balance is calculated by subtracting the payments and any credits from the balance owed at the end of the previous billing period.

*3.  Previous Balance Method*

This is the most expensive method. The finance charge is calculated on the balance owed at the end of the previous billing cycle. Payments, credits and new purchases made in the current billing cycle are not included.

*4.  Credit Availability*

The credit availability will depend on the following considerations:

- Age: Must be 18 to obtain a credit card.
- Income: Must have an income or assets.
- Amount: The amount must be realistic, based on the income and any credit already had.
- Purpose: It should be for a good reason, such as a student loan. Credit Card Responsibilities With the first purchase on a credit card, the holder have entered into a legal agreement with the credit card company.

*5.  Responsibilities*

Some other responsibilities are:

- To keep cards in a safe place.
- do not give the credit card number to friends.
- before signing receipts, verify for accuracy.
- destroy all carbon copies.
- keep all receipts to check against the billing statement.
- inform the credit card company immediately if lost.
- become familiar with the consumer credit laws that protects.
- A mini-lesson titled Women and Credit Laws will give the information about the key provisions.

## Advantages of Using a Credit Card

Being able to spread the cost of purchases, the biggest advantage that credit cards have over debit cards is the financial protection they offer in the event something goes wrong. Under a combination of the Consumer Credit Act and Consumer Credit Directive, if card used to buy something and it turns out to be faulty or the company goes bust, the money is received back from the card provider.

- Allows shopping or traveling without carrying large sums of cash. Most cards are accepted all over the world.
- Can give immediate use of the goods and services, which is especially important for expensive items like appliances and furniture.
- Can be used to deal with unexpected financial emergencies.
- Can help to track how much spent by giving a record of purchases.
- Can offer protection against theft. If card is lost or stolen and to notify the credit card company immediately, the most typically be liable for is Rs.50 of the unauthorized spending. Many companies currently waive this fee, however.

## Disadvantages of Credit Cards

- Purchases may cost more if not paid in full at the end of the month. Interest and other charges are added to the purchase price of goods and services.
- Ties up future income. When credit used and the inv owe money that must be paid back from income you have not yet earned. This may make it more difficult to deal with unexpected events and emergencies.
- Can encourage overspending. You may buy more than you holder can pay for, and may even buy things not needed.
- Can lead to major financial problems if poorly managed.

# 12. ORIGINATIONS

## Origination-Meaning

Origination is the process of creating a home loan or mortgage. During the origination process, a borrower submits a variety of financial information, tax returns, prior paychecks, credit card info, bank balances, etc. to the mortgage lender, who uses it to determine the type of loan the borrower is eligible for and what interest rate he or she will pay. The lender will also rely on the borrower's credit report and other information to determine loan eligibility.

Origination is the process of making or initiating a new loan. Origination involves being the initial contact to a consumer and taking a loan application. It can also involve ordering a credit report and assembling all of the other forms and documents required by the person or company who is underwriting the loan.

Loan Origination policies and procedures is designed to provide step-by-step guidance. It keeps loan officers in compliance, provides quality control in the process, and establishes guidelines for federal laws. In addition to insuring quality loan applications, it also defines procedures for avoiding fraud, predatory lending and ethics violations. Finally, this acts as a procedural training guide for mortgage loan officers and originators. In those states that require it, this provides the required written supervisory plan required of lenders.

## Origination Elements

- Lending Operations.
- Anti-Predatory Lending.
- Fair Lending.
- Marketing Policies and Procedures.
- Federal Compliance.
- Position Descriptions.
- Compensation.
- Lock-in policies.
- Pricing Policies.
- Lock-in Completion.
- Pre-qualifying.
- Pre-Approval.
- Marketing Material Policy.
- Complete Application Process.
- Completing good faith estimate.
- Setting up loan files for processing.
- Pipeline review.
- Closing preparation procedures.
- Predatory Lending Policy.
- Ethical Mortgage Lending Practices.
- Complaint Resolution Process.

## Loan Processing

A loan processor works on the file assembled by the originator. The processor is typically responsible for verification of the information contained in the file (such as sending out employment verification forms) and also coordination of the various aspects of the loan (such as working with the title company).

## Underwriting

Underwriting is the process of evaluating and deciding whether to make a new loan and, if yes, on what terms. This is done by the funding source-usually an investor, depository, or mortgage lender, but never by a mortgage broker, who only originates loans for lenders.

Underwriting involves evaluating credit scores, credit history, appraisals, job history, and other measures of strength or weakness in the borrower and the collateral. There are specific skills and expertise required for this function that go beyond simply evaluating numbers produced by a computer. Additional experience and training are required in this area.

## Servicing

Servicing is the continued maintenance of a loan after the loan has closed. This can be done, for example, by a lender, a servicing company set up solely to perform this function, or some other acceptable entity.

Servicing involves maintaining direct contact with borrowers, sending mortgage and escrow analysis statements, collecting payments, and pursuing late payments. Often, a primary lender will sell a mortgage to the secondary market, but still service the loan for a fee.

Many mortgage companies offer a combination of these functions to their clients. For one loan, they may provide all of the services: Originate the loan (find the borrower), underwrite the loan (evaluate the borrower), and service the loan (continue to interact with the borrower). If the lender is not able to provide a loan product that meets the needs of a particular borrower, the lender may simply act as a broker and assist in finding another lender in order to earn an origination fee.

## Loan Processing

Generally speaking, with today's federal disclosure requirements, borrowers should complete a loan application only when they are ready to buy a particular home. Even if the borrower is not ready to make an offer on the house, the borrower may be pre-qualified. This is not the same as pre-approving buyers. The two terms are not interchangeable, so it is important to thoroughly understand the differences between them.

### Pre-Qualification

Pre-qualification is the process of pre-determining how much a potential borrower might be eligible to borrow. This may be done by any mortgage loan originator, but it does not guarantee approval. Pre-qualification of a buyer is not binding on the mortgage broker or lender-which is why the distinction is important. It is a free "test run" of the loan application process that usually takes only a few hours. The mortgage broker or lender is only saying that it looks favorable that the borrower will be approved. Often there's more background research, documentation, and information that the mortgage broker or lender must obtain, but won't until the borrower has actually applied for the loan. However, if the lender renders a credit decision, the pre-qualification becomes an application and the required disclosures will need to be delivered. The pre-qualification process involves asking prospective borrowers questions about income and debts. A credit report may be pulled by a MLO, or the borrower may just be asked questions about his or her financial situation. A mortgage loan originator's pre-qualification of a prospective borrower may be as simple as making sure that the borrower has a steady job and no glaring credit report problems, like a recent bankruptcy. Often, a MLO will compute the borrower's income and debt ratios to get an idea of how much house a prospective buyer may be able to afford. Some lenders or mortgage brokers offer a loan pre-qualification certificate form, which is not binding. Assuming a credit decision is not anticipated as a result of this, it does not trigger required disclosures. MLOs may also provide a closing cost worksheet while the loan is still in the pre-qualification state. If such a worksheet is provided, however, it must become a part of the loan file once it becomes a formal application.

*Pre-Approval*

Pre-approval is the process by which a lender determines if potential borrowers can be financed through the lender, and for what amount of money. They are rendering a credit decision. Generally speaking, a mortgage broker cannot give a borrower a pre-approval; only the lender can pre-approve. For a pre-approval, a borrower goes through most of the same steps in the loan process, such as completing an application and providing documentation of income and assets. With a pre-approval, a lender is stating that the prospective borrower's situation has been investigated and, provided all circumstances stay the same, the lender is willing to loan a certain amount of money to purchase a house. This is especially helpful when working with buyers because it is a powerful negotiation tool in getting an offer accepted by a seller and, in most cases, is a requirement of contract acceptance. Of course, a borrower's circumstances can and do change which is why there are always conditions listed on a pre-approval. Depending upon internal pre-approval procedures, some pre-approvals are more specific and binding. This is where experience is helpful, and where to take advantage of the wisdom and experience of the employer and other senior mortgage professionals can offer. Pre-approvals are always in writing and always follow the policies and procedures established by the employer or mortgage lender. Completing an application in anticipation of a credit decision triggers federally mandated disclosures, which includes a Good Faith Estimate of closing costs (GFE) and a Truth in Lending Statement (both of which will be discussed in detail in the next chapter). In order to submit a loan application for pre-approval, the borrower must be given a GFE, which binds the MLO to its terms. While the Department of Housing and Urban Development (HUD) allows a borrower to be pre-approved without identifying a specific property address, mortgage loan originators are not required to provide a GFE under such circumstances.

## Traditional Steps

The loan approval process traditionally consists of four steps, including:

1. Consulting with the mortgage loan originator
2. Completing a loan application
3. Processing a loan application
4. Analyzing the borrower and property

*Consulting with the Mortgage Loan Originator*

Whether a prospective borrower wishes to consult with a mortgage loan originator in person or online, the first step to choose the right one. If a borrower already has a relationship with a MLO, this may be a good place to start. On the other hand, if a borrower has past credit problems, it may be helpful to use a mortgage company that deals with many different lenders, although in today's tight market and stringent credit score qualifying standards, this is not the fix for credit issues it once was.

As borrowers decide how to proceed with applying for their loan, remember these points:

- Do not interject the opinion into the situation. This is especially important if a MLO representing many different lenders and loan programs.
- Always let clients or customers have the final say as to how they apply for a loan and with whom.
- If worked with more than one investor or company program, always consult with the Mortgage Company or employer regarding the policies in all areas before giving any type of advice or recommendation. After the lender is selected, initial discussions usually involve the various types of mortgages it offers so the borrower can decide which loan best suits his or her needs. A borrower will need to give the lender a good deal of personal and financial data on which the lender will base the lending decision. Providing the borrower with a complete list of required documents and reviewing these documents early in the application will help speed up the approval process.

## *Interest Rates*

One topic that inevitably arises very early in a borrower's conversations with a MLO is the interest rate that may be available. The interest rate is the amount charged by a lender to a borrower for the use of assets, expressed as a percentage of the loan amount (the principal). A couple of other terms to keep in mind when discussing interest with borrowers:

- **Par Rate**: Par rate is a term that describes the rate without discounts or points that lenders offer only to mortgage brokers, also known as the "wholesale" rate, that does not create an additional charge or provide for a credit for the borrower.
- **Rate Lock**: This is a commitment guaranteed by a lender that an interest rate will not change on a specific loan for a specific period of time. Since a lock-in agreement generally requires that the loan close by a specific date, the anticipated close date should be carefully considered. If a loan closes after the rate lock expires, the lender may choose to offer the market rate current at that time or the original lock-in rate.
- **Float**: Between the time of application and closing, a borrower may choose to bet on interest rates decreasing by electing to float. Floating is essentially choosing not to lock the interest rate. Since it is the borrower's responsibility to lock his or her rate before closing, choosing to float is considered risky and may result in a higher interest rate.

## *Common Fees Associated with Real Estate Loans*

In addition to the interest, there are other fees associated with processing a real estate loan, for example, fees for pulling a borrower's credit bureau report, securing a property appraisal report, and for completing inspections. Other items like title insurance and recording fees are paid if and when a loan closes. Fees that occur only when a loan closes are likely to be paid out of closing funds, but other early expenses incurred must be paid, even if the loan doesn't close. A prior relationship with a mortgage loan originator can help when discussing fees, because the MLO may agree to absorb some smaller costs, such as for the credit report. More costly items, such as a property appraisal, may have to be paid for by the borrower before a final underwriting decision is made.

## *Loan Origination Fees*

For loans that actually close, lenders charge a loan origination fee to cover the administrative costs of making and processing the loan, including setting up the loan on the lender's books. Such fees may be referred to collectively as points. A point is simply one percent of the loan amount. Points can be charged for many reasons, such as closing fees, underwriting fees, documentation fees, etc., but all points serve to help increase the lender's return. Mortgage loan originators base loan fees on what the market will bear. Another factor the lender considers when determining the number of points charged on a loan is the sale of the loan on the secondary market. For example, a lender may need to sell a loan at a discount to compensate that secondary market buyer for the time value of money. The lender can attempt to make up some of any loss by charging the borrower points. Alternatively, in a competitive environment, some of those fees may even be waived as the lender can sell the loan in the secondary market at a premium. It all depends on the current market and rate of the loan.

## Differences between an Underwriter and a Processor

Loan underwriters and processors serve an important function in the process of evaluating and approving loans and distributing their proceeds. After a loan application is completed and submitted, the loan processor reviews the loan application and attached documentation for completeness and accuracy. A loan underwriter evaluates the information on a loan application against various lending standards to determine if the applicant should receive the loan amount requested. These two positions make it possible for a lender to make loans and for a borrower to obtain the funds needed for her business.

### *Loan Underwriting Responsibilities*

A loan underwriter's job responsibilities include performing a detailed credit analysis of a borrower. The underwriter looks at a borrower's employment record, income sources and credit report. A borrower's credit score, the amount of debt he carries and his payment history are other critical pieces of information an underwriter also considers. An underwriter determines if a borrower's financial ratios, such as debt-to-income ratio, meet the bank's lending standards. For collateral loans, the underwriter is responsible for evaluating the condition of the asset and determining that the borrower has or will get good title to the asset.

### *Underwriter Job Requirements*

Various job requirements need to be met to work as an underwriter. First and foremost, an underwriter must be a person with an attention for financial details and be able to understand established lending requirements. Familiarity with federal and industry standards and the ability to apply them on a case-by-case basis is also necessary. An underwriter must also be extremely analytical, be able to evaluate the financial information presented to her and demonstrate some flexibility in applying lending criteria. The job also requires a person who is a team player, has effective communication skills and excellent customer service skills. Loan underwriters often have bachelor's degrees in business or finance or related areas, although this is not a rigid requirement. Mortgage loan underwriters must also be licensed.

### *Loan Processing Responsibilities*

A loan processor organizes the loan application's documentation and makes sure it's in order before the underwriter reviews the loan file. The processor typically contacts the borrower if information is missing or if additional information or documentation is required. She must review the documents received and determine if they comply with the lender's standards. A loan processor's responsibilities are less rigorous than the underwriter's because the processor does not decide on loan approval. Her review for completeness and accuracy of the loan file makes the underwriter's job easier.

### *Processor Job Requirements*

The job requirements to become a loan processor are less extensive than those for an underwriter. Good organizational skills are necessary to handle the substantial amount of documentation that makes up a loan file. Educational requirements include a high school diploma, but a college degree is not necessary. Many lenders and banks also train loan processors on applicable internal and external guidelines and procedures.

## Strategic Importance of Credit Card Payments

Developing a payments strategy can help merchants better plan for the future, keep pace with their competitors, and maximize their financial performance. Below are additional considerations for merchants that are developing and implementing their payments strategy. Benefits for Merchants and Consumers Along with the easier-to-measure costs associated with accepting electronic payments, credit and debit offer a number of benefits to merchants.

### Advantages

1. Greater revenues: according to industry research, average transaction amounts tend to be higher when using electronic payments.
2. Improved security over cash, since cards reduce the amount of on-site cash and related cash theft.
3. Reduced costs associated with handling cash.
4. Improved reporting compared with cash, with some acquirers offering online access to information such as recent transactions, adjustments and bank deposits for a range of time periods (i.e., daily, weekly, monthly, etc.). Strong reporting provides merchants with increased visibility into their business, which can aid in planning. Consumers are turning more to credit and debit cards mainly due to convenience. Customer comfort levels and perceptions of speed for credit and debit cards are similar to cash. For credit cards, buyers can take advantage of getting access to a line of credit on demand.

Meanwhile, debit cards offer consumers quick access to their checking accounts without having to write a check. And many consumers prefer to use debit rather than credit to better manage their spending and not add to a revolving balance.

### Understanding the Payments Mix

Merchants can take steps to lower their payments-related costs while maintaining or increasing their revenues. Directing customers to a particular payment type seems to be the preferred method among some merchants. For example, steering customers to lower cost PIN debit generally saves merchants money (compared with signature debit), while still offering customers the convenience of debt payments. Merchants can implement different approaches to encourage customers to pay with a particular payment type:

1. **Rewards Programs**: Coffee houses and fuel merchants have been the most aggressive in guiding their customers to use gift cards and certain types of debit card products through targeted rewards. Rewards programs can serve the dual purpose of lowering payments costs and increasing revenues, although, at least some of the cost savings are applied to maintenance of the rewards program.
2. **Consumers have choices at the POS**: Some merchants take steps to guide customers to PIN debit by first presenting customers with a PIN option; to conduct a signature based transaction, the user must cancel the screen then search for the option on a subsequent screen.

## What to Look for in a Provider

Knowing what to look for in a provider of credit and debit card acceptance products and services can help merchants stand apart from their competitors, maximize revenues, and minimize troublesome issues.

### i.	Security

Now more than ever, merchants need to make sure providers are aware of the latest security trends. A provider should work closely with merchants and financial institutions to help address risk and fraud across the entire customer life cycle with a comprehensive set of prevention and detection solutions.

It should offer customized, innovative solutions that enable merchants to stay ahead of trends to effectively manage risk and to detect, prevent and reduce fraud. That includes tools that help prevent credit and debit card fraud, facilitate PCI compliance and offer transaction data protection solutions. Merchants should also work with a provider that helps ensure compliance with all industry encryption standards for the transmission of data. The vendor should also be knowledgeable about standards such as the PCI DSS and Payment Application Data Security Standard (PA DSS). And the provider should be able to work easily with third parties to provide the tools necessary to support merchant compliance.

## ii.    Reliability

Whether a cardholder is purchasing a gift on the busiest shopping day of the year or buying tickets to a play right before the opening act, providers need to get it right the first time. Vendors should have multiple flexible processing platforms and full data-center redundancy for maximum uptime reliability.

## iii.    Relevant Expertise and Expert Advice

A provider should have dedicated account relationship management teams with specialized expertise, so that they can best serve the merchant type and the issues it faces. The provider should proactively work with clients to identify issues as they arise and develop an action plan for resolution. It should also analyze a client's business for potential savings and growth opportunities. The vendor should have a staff with deep knowledge of historical and future payments trends. The provider should also always follow through and often exceed a merchant's expectation across the gamut of issues, including escalations, funding questions, chargeback inquiries, transaction/batch questions and the like. In addition, they should provide a timely explanation of compliance mandates and be their merchants' advocate within the industry.

## iv.    Portfolio Solutions that Meet Business Needs

A provider should offer competitive rates, transaction security, flexible billing and timely, accurate reporting options. A vendor should have a full range of POS terminals, peripherals and supplies designed to save both time and money while supporting all Payment Card Industry (PCI) compliance standards. The vendor should have flexible payment acceptance options, including credit, debit, check, gift card, Electronic Benefits. Merchants should have full access to their account information through robust, web-based reporting tools and solutions to help them simplify back-office processes and expedite response time.

## Credit Card Reconciliation

Credit card reconciliations are the process of verifying the integrity of data between credit card statements or other associated reports from merchant services providers and a company's internal financial records. Credit card reconciliation begins with the comparison of transactions between credit card statements and the associated transactions within various accounts in a company's chart of accounts. This is a necessary step to ensure that credit card statements and balances are correct and accurate. Accountants then investigate any discrepancies found and take necessary corrective action.

### Process for Credit Card Reconciliation

The credit card reconciliation process is carried out when credit card statements are initially received or after the close of a financial period. Accountants go through each transaction on the credit card statement and match it to transactions in the company's internal systems.

This includes both outbound credit card payments to suppliers and service providers and inbound credit card payments from customers. When discrepancies are found, investigation is performed to determine the appropriate corrective action.

Corrective action may involve disputing transactions with the credit card processor, making journal entries to correct timing items or errors, or other actions to address transaction issues. A company may have a limited time to dispute transactions such as charge backs with a merchant services provider, so speed and accuracy are paramount in this process.

All research performed, information found, and actions taken are stored for audit purposes. For companies with large amounts of credit card transactions, the credit card reconciliation process is a key step in the verification of financial data.

## Purchasing Card Policy and Procedures

### Purpose and Goals

The Purchasing Card program provides an efficient, cost effective method of purchasing and paying for small dollar transactions. The program is designed to reduce numerous processes including petty cash, low dollar checks, cash advances, and small-dollar purchase orders. These procedures provide the guidelines for use of a department purchasing card.

### Using the card

At least one person in each department have a Purchasing Card and all departments are encouraged to use their Purchasing Cards. The Purchasing Card eliminates the need to submit requisitions and obtain purchase orders, subsequently reducing repetitive tasks and paperwork. All Purchasing Card holders must comply with these guidelines and holders may be personally responsible for charges not in compliance with these guidelines.

### Restrictions

The card may not be used for items on contracts, or any products or services considered an inappropriate use of funds. The following items are prohibited but should not be considered a complete list:

- Alcoholic beverages.
- Gift cards.
- Gifts/prizes/greeting cards.
- Cash advances.
- Charitable contributions.
- Firearms.
- Flowers for individual employees.
- Furniture (any kind).
- Hazardous chemicals and radioactive materials.
- Political contributions.
- Prescription drugs.
- Renovation/construction services.
- Security systems.
- Software.
- Vehicles.

## Billing Reconciliation and Verification

Departments are responsible for monthly reconciliation of their card statements. The monthly cardholder statement will detail charges made during the previous billing cycle. This information must be reviewed promptly for accuracy.

## Monthly Reconciliation

Reconciliation worksheet: A reconciliation worksheet to facilitate and standardize record-keeping for the required monthly reconciliation is to be developed.

## Reconciliation Process

- The cardholder is required to reconcile each charge on the statement to the corresponding original receipt, each month within seven days of receipt of the statement.
- The monthly statement and all original receipts corresponding to transactions listed thereon are to be attached to the Purchasing Card reconciliation worksheet (PDF).
- The business purpose of each expense should be noted in the space provided on the reconciliation worksheet.
- If the recipient of the goods and/or services is different than the cardholder, then the recipient should sign the receipt, packing slip, or other documentation.
- The cardholder and supervisor must sign and date both the reconciliation worksheet and the monthly statement. If there were no purchases during the month and therefore no statement, add a note to that effect to the reconciliation worksheet.

## Recordkeeping

After reconciliation is complete, all Purchasing Card monthly statements, receipts and monthly reconciliation worksheets must be kept by departments in their files for a period from the date of statement.

Periodic audits of Purchasing Card activities and record keeping will be conducted by the Controller's Office to ensure compliance to the Purchasing Card program terms and conditions listed in this document.

## Expense Categorization

Each month the cardholder should review expenses online and assign any charges to the appropriate budget numbers (charges will be assigned to a default budget number, as provided on a Purchasing Card application, when transactions are posted on a Purchasing Card account). The cardholder has the option to perform an on-line reassignment of budget accounts from a default to other more appropriate accounts. The cardholder will have up to 5 days after the close of the billing cycle to do on-line reassignments.

## Grants

If using credit card for purchases funded by sponsored research funds, must adhere to the Grant's Office and awarding agency's policies, restrictions and guidelines.

## Disputing a Charge

Disputed billing can result from failure to receive goods or services, fraud, incorrect amounts, duplicate charges, etc. The cardholder should contact the supplier first to resolve any outstanding issues. Note that, by law, suppliers are not allowed to bill the card for purchases until the items have been shipped.

*Returning Items*

It is essential that the supplier be contacted for a return authorization. Items should be returned directly to the supplier by whichever means the supplier requires. Retain supporting documentation on file. The cardholder is responsible for ensuring that proper credit is posted for any returned item(s).

*Termination/Cancellation of the Purchasing Card*

Purchasing cards may be cancelled if a department or individual does not comply with policies and procedures stated in this document.

## Cardholder Dispute

A cardholder dispute occurs when there is a disagreement with a merchant about a charge. The following are examples of disputes:

1. When a transaction is cancelled with a merchant, but the merchant charged anyway.
2. When an item purchased with debit card and later returned the item to the merchant; however the account was not credited.
3. Charged twice for the same purchase.
4. Attempted to withdraw funds at an ATM, but the cash was not disbursed from the machine and the account was debited.
5. When card used to "hold" a purchase, than paid for the purchase using another method of payment, and the debit card was also charged.
6. Charged an incorrect amount for a transaction.
7. When theirs is an issue with the quality of the goods or services provided.

*How to Process Dispute*

Timely notice is critical! Regulation requires that to notify the credit union within two business days of the date first become aware of the transaction. Failure to notify us within two business days increases the liability. If not notified within sixty days from when the transaction appeared on statement, the holder is liable for the entire amount of the disputed transaction. What needed from the process to claim:

1. Cardholder Dispute Form
2. Statement of Occurrence
3. All documentation supporting the transaction and the attempt to first work out the dispute with the merchant.

*Fraudulent Transactions*

A fraudulent transaction occurs only when the holder have no knowledge of who used the card and can state with certainty that were not aware of the transaction. The holder must notify the credit union within two business days upon discovering fraud and will be required to sign an affidavit attesting to the fact that the holders have no knowledge of who completed the transactions in question. The credit union reserves the right the required to complete a police report if deemed it necessary for the investigation. The holder is responsible for all transactions the authorized, using Debit Card if voluntarily permitted someone else to use the card or PIN number. What needed to process the fraud claim is:

1. Cardholder Fraudulent Transaction Dispute Form.
2. Statement of Occurrence.
3. Signed Affidavit.

# 13.  MORTGAGE

## Introduction

A **mortgage loan**, also referred to as a **mortgage**, is used by purchasers of real property to raise funds to buy real estate; by existing property owners to raise funds for any purpose while putting a lien on the property being mortgaged. The loan is "secured" on the borrower's property. This means that a legal mechanism is put in place which allows the lender to take possession and sell the secured property ("foreclosure" or "repossession") to pay off the loan in the event that the borrower defaults on the loan or otherwise fails to abide by its terms. The word *mortgage* is derived from a "Law French" term used by English lawyers in the Middle Ages meaning "death pledge", and refers to the pledge ending (dying) when either the obligation is fulfilled or the property is taken through foreclosure. Mortgage can also be described as "a borrower giving consideration in the form of a collateral for a benefit.

Mortgages make larger purchases possible for individuals lacking enough cash to purchase an asset, like a house, up front. Lenders take a risk making these loans as there is no guarantee the borrower will be able to pay in the future. Borrowers take risk in accepting these loans, as a failure to pay will result in a total loss of the asset.

A mortgage is a debt instrument, secured by the collateral of specified real estate property that the borrower is obliged to pay back with a predetermined set of payments. Mortgages are used by individuals and businesses to make large real estate purchases without paying the entire value of the purchase up front. Over a period of many years, the borrower repays the loan, plus interest, until he/she eventually owns the property free and clear. Mortgages are also known as "liens against property" or "claims on property." If the borrower stops paying the mortgage, the bank can foreclose.

A mortgage is a loan in which property or real estate is used as collateral. The borrower enters into an agreement with the lender (usually a bank) wherein the borrower receives cash upfront then makes payments over a set time span until he pays back the lender in full. In a residential mortgage, a home buyer pledges his or her house to the bank. The bank has a claim on the house should the home buyer default on paying the mortgage. In the case of a foreclosure, the bank may evict the home's tenants and sell the house, using the income from the sale to clear the mortgage debt.

Mortgages come in many forms. With a fixed-rate mortgage, the borrower pays the same interest rate for the life of the loan. Her monthly principal and interest payment never change from the first mortgage payment to the last. Most fixed-rate mortgages have a 15 or 30-year term. If market interest rates rise, the borrower's payment does not change. If market interest rates drop significantly, the borrower may be able to secure that lower rate by refinancing the mortgage. A fixed-rate mortgage is also called a "traditional" mortgage.

Mortgages are like any other financial product in that their supply and demand will change dependent on the market. For that reason, sometimes banks can offer very low interest rates and sometimes only the bank can only offer high rates. If a borrower agreed upon a high interest rate and finds after a few years that rates have dropped, he can sign a new agreement at the new lower interest rate after jumping though some hoops, of course. This is called "refinancing."

## Basic Concepts and Legal Regulation

According to Anglo-American property law, a mortgage occurs when an owner pledges his or her right to the property as security or collateral for a loan. Therefore, a mortgage is an encumbrance on the right to the property just as an easement would be, but because most mortgages occur as a condition for new loan money, the word *mortgage* has become the generic term for a loan secured by such real property. As with other types of loans, mortgages have an interest rate and are scheduled to amortize over a set period of time, typically 30 years. All types of real property can be, and usually are, secured with a mortgage and bear an interest rate that is supposed to reflect the lender's risk. Mortgage lending is the primary mechanism used in many countries to finance private ownership of residential and commercial property. Although the terminology and precise forms will differ from country to country, the basic components tend to be similar:

Many other specific characteristics are common to many markets, but the above are the essential features. Governments usually regulate many aspects of mortgage lending, either directly through legal requirements or indirectly through regulation of the participants or the financial markets, such as the banking industry, and often through state intervention like direct lending by the government, by state-owned banks, or sponsorship of various entities. Other aspects that define a specific mortgage market may be regional, historical, or driven by specific characteristics of the legal or financial system.

Mortgage loans are generally structured as long-term loans, the periodic payments for which are similar to an annuity and calculated according to the time value of money formulae. The most basic arrangement would require a fixed monthly payment over a period of ten to thirty years, depending on local conditions. Over this period the principal component of the loan would be slowly paid down through amortization. In practice, many variants are possible and common worldwide and within each country.

Lenders provide funds against property to earn interest income, and generally borrow these funds themselves (for example, by taking deposits or issuing bonds). The price at which the lenders borrow money therefore affects the cost of borrowing. Lenders may also, in many countries, sell the mortgage loan to other parties who are interested in receiving the stream of cash payments from the borrower, often in the form of a security(by means of a securitization).

Mortgage lending will also take into account the (perceived) riskiness of the mortgage loan, that is, the likelihood that the funds will be repaid (usually considered a function of the creditworthiness of the borrower); that if not repaid, the lender will be able to foreclose on the real estate assets; and the financial, interest rate risk and time delays that may be involved in certain circumstances.

## Loan and Mortgage Terminology

Several terms are commonly used when discussing loans and mortgages. It is important to understand them before borrowing or lending.

- **Principal**: The amount borrowed that has yet to be repaid, minus any interest. For example, if someone has taken out a Rs.5,000 loan and paid back Rs.3,000, the principal is Rs.2,000. It does not take into account any interest that might be due on top of the remaining Rs.2,000 owed.
- **Interest:** A "fee" charged by a creditor for a debtor to borrow money. Interest payments greatly incentivize creditors to take on the financial risk of lending money, as the ideal scenario results in a creditor earning back all the money loaned, plus some percentage above that; this makes for a good return on investment (ROI).

- **Interest Rate:** The rate at which a percentage of the principal - the amount of a loan yet owed - is repaid, with interest, within a certain period of time. It is calculated by dividing the principal by the amount of interest.
- **Annual Percentage Rate (APR):** The costs of a loan over the course of a year, including any and all interest, insurance or origination fees.
- **Pre-qualified:** Pre-qualification for a loan is a statement from a financial institution that provides a non-binding and approximate estimate of the amount a person is eligible to borrow.
- **Pre-approved:** Pre-approval for a loan is the first step of a formal loan application. The lender verifies the borrower's credit rating and income before pre-approval.
- **Down Payment:** Cash a borrower gives to a lender upfront as part of an initial loan repayment. The mortgage loan would cover the remaining costs and be paid back, with interest, over time.
- **Lien:** Something used to secure loans, especially mortgages; the legal right a lender has to a property or asset, should the borrower default on loan repayments.
- **Private Mortgage Insurance (PMI):** Some borrowers-those who use either an FHA loan, or a conventional loan with a down payment of less than 20% are required to purchase mortgage insurance, which protects the borrower's ability to keep making mortgage payments. Premiums for mortgage insurance are paid monthly and usually bundled with the monthly mortgage payments, just like homeowner's insurance and property taxes.
- **Prepayment:** Paying a loan in part or in full before its due date. Some lenders actually penalize borrowers with an interest fee for early repayment as it causes lenders to lose out on interest charges that might have been able to make had the borrower kept the loan for a longer time.
- **Foreclosure:** The legal right and process a lender uses to recoup financial losses incurred from having a borrower fail to repay a loan; usually results in a public auction of the asset that was used for collateral, with proceeds going toward the mortgage debt.
- **Property:** The physical residence being financed. The exact form of ownership will vary from country to country, and may restrict the types of lending that are possible.
- **Mortgage:** The security interest of the lender in the property, which may entail restrictions on the use or disposal of the property. Restrictions may include requirements to purchase home insurance and mortgage insurance, or pay off outstanding debt before selling the property.
- **Borrower:** The person borrowing who either has or is creating an ownership interest in the property.
- **Lender:** Any lender, but usually a bank or other financial institution. (In some countries, particularly the United States, Lenders may also be investors who own an interest in the mortgage through a mortgage-backed security. In such a situation, the initial lender is known as the mortgage originator, which then packages and sells the loan to investors. The payments from the borrower are thereafter collected by a loan servicer.

## Types of Mortgage Loans

Mortgage loans are usually entered into by home buyers without enough cash on hand to purchase the home. The borrower are also used to borrow cash from a bank for other projects using their house as collateral. There are several types of mortgage loans and buyers should assess what is best for their own situation before entering into one. Types of loans are characterized by their term dates, interest rates, and the amount of payments per period.

The two basic types of amortized loans are:

a. The fixed rate mortgage (FRM) and
b. Adjustable-Rate Mortgage (ARM) (also known as a floating rate or variable rate mortgage).

   Combinations of fixed and floating rate mortgages are common, whereby a mortgage loan will have a fixed rate for some period, for example the first five years, and vary after the end of that period.

   - In a **fixed rate mortgage**, the interest rate, remains fixed for the life (or term) of the loan. In case of an annuity repayment scheme, the periodic payment remains the same amount throughout the loan. In case of linear payback, the periodic payment will gradually decrease.

   - In an **adjustable rate mortgage**, the interest rate is generally fixed for a period of time, after which it will periodically (for example, annually or monthly) adjust up or down to some market index. The initial interest rate is often a below-market rate, which can make a mortgage seem more affordable than it really is. Adjustable rates transfer part of the interest rate risk from the lender to the borrower, and thus are widely used where fixed rate funding is difficult to obtain or prohibitively expensive. If interest rates increase later, the borrower may not be able to afford the higher monthly payments. Interest rates could also decrease, making an ARM less expensive. In either case, the monthly payments are unpredictable after the initial term.

c. Individuals mortgaging their home can be businesses mortgaging commercial property. The lender will typically be a financial institution, such as a bank, credit union or building society, depending on the country concerned, and the loan arrangements can be made either directly or indirectly through intermediaries. Features of mortgage loans such as the size of the loan, maturity of the loan, interest rate, method of paying off the loan, and other characteristics can vary considerably. The lender's rights over the secured property take priority over the borrower's other creditors which means that if the borrower becomes bankrupt or insolvent, the other creditors will only be repaid the debts owed to them from a sale of the secured property if the mortgage lender is repaid in full first.

In many jurisdictions, though not all, it is normal for home purchases to be funded by a mortgage loan. Few individuals have enough savings or liquid funds to enable them to purchase property outright. In countries where the demand for home ownership is highest, strong domestic markets for mortgages have developed.

## Mortgage Underwriting

Once the mortgage application enters into the final steps, the loan application is moved to a Mortgage Underwriter. The Underwriter verifies the financial information that the applicant has provided to the lender. Verification will be made for the applicant's credit history and the value of the home being purchased. An appraisal may be ordered. The financial and employment information of the applicant will also be verified.

The underwriting may take a few days to a few weeks. Sometimes the underwriting process takes so long that the provided financial statements need to be resubmitted are current. It is advisable to maintain the same employment and not to use or open new credit during the underwriting process. Any changes made in the applicant's credit, employment, or financial information can result in the loan being denied.

The charge to the borrower depends upon the credit risk in addition to the interest rate risk. The mortgage origination and underwriting process involves checking credit scores, debt-to-income, down payments, and assets. Jumbo mortgages and subprime lending are not supported by government guarantees and face higher interest rates. Other innovations described below can affect the rates as well.

## Loan to Value and Down Payments

Upon making a mortgage loan for the purchase of a property, lenders usually require that the borrower make a down payment; that is, contribute a portion of the cost of the property. This down payment may be expressed as a portion of the value of the property. The loan to value ratio is the size of the loan against the value of the property. For loans made against properties that the borrower already owns, the loan to value ratio will be imputed against the estimated value of the property. The loan to value ratio is considered an important indicator of the riskiness of a mortgage loan: the higher the LTV, the higher the risk that the value of the property will be insufficient to cover the remaining principal of the loan.

## Value: Appraised, Estimated and Actual

Since the value of the property is an important factor in understanding the risk of the loan, determining the value is a key factor in mortgage lending. The value may be determined in various ways, but the most common are:

1. *Actual or transaction value*: this is usually taken to be the purchase price of the property. If the property is not being purchased at the time of borrowing, this information may not be available.
2. *Appraised or surveyed value*: in most jurisdictions, some form of appraisal of the value by a licensed professional is common. There is often a requirement for the lender to obtain an official appraisal.
3. *Estimated value*: lenders or other parties may use their own internal estimates, particularly in jurisdictions where no official appraisal procedure exists, but also in some other circumstances.

## Payment and Debt Ratios

In most countries, a number of more or less standard measures of creditworthiness may be used. Common measures include payment to income (mortgage payments as a percentage of gross or net income); debt to income (all debt payments, including mortgage payments, as a percentage of income); and various net worth measures. In many countries, credit scores are used in lieu of or to supplement these measures. There will also be requirements for documentation of the creditworthiness, such as income tax returns, pay stubs, etc. the specifics will vary from location to location.

Some lenders may also require a potential borrower have one or more months of "reserve assets" available. In other words, the borrower may be required to show the availability of enough assets to pay for the housing costs (including mortgage, taxes, etc.) for a period of time in the event of the job loss or other loss of income.

Many countries have lower requirements for certain borrowers, or "no-doc" or "low-doc" lending standards that may be acceptable under certain circumstances.

*Standard or Conforming Mortgages*

Many countries have a notion of standard or conforming mortgages that define a perceived acceptable level of risk, which may be formal or informal, and may be reinforced by laws, government intervention, or market practice.

A standard or conforming mortgage is a key concept as it often defines whether or not the mortgage can be easily sold or securitized, or, if non-standard, may affect the price at which it may be sold. In the United States, a conforming mortgage is one which meets the established rules and procedures of the two major government-sponsored entities in the housing finance market. In contrast, lenders who decide to make nonconforming loans are exercising a higher risk tolerance and do so knowing that the borrower face more challenge in reselling the loan. Many countries have similar concepts or agencies that define what are "standard" mortgages. Regulated lenders (such as banks) may be subject to limits or higher risk weightings for non-standard mortgages. For example, banks and mortgage brokerages in Canada face restrictions on lending more than 80% of the property value; beyond this level, mortgage insurance is generally required.

*Foreign Currency Mortgage*

In some countries with currencies that tend to depreciate, foreign currency mortgages are common, enabling lenders to lend in a stable foreign currency, whilst the borrower takes on the currency risk that the currency will depreciate and will therefore need to convert higher amounts of the domestic currency to repay the loan.

## Repaying the Mortgage

In addition to the two standard means of setting the *cost* of a mortgage loan (fixed at a set interest rate for the term, or variable relative to market interest rates), there are variations in *how* that cost is paid, and how the loan itself is repaid. Repayment depends on locality, tax laws and prevailing culture. There are also various mortgage repayment structures to suit different types of borrower.

*Principal and Interest*

The most common way to repay a secured mortgage loan is to make regular payments toward the principal and interest over a set term. This is commonly referred to as amortization and as a repayment mortgage. A mortgage is a form of annuity, and the calculation of the periodic payments is based on the time value of money. Certain details may be specific to different locations: interest may be calculated on the basis of a 360-day of a year or may be compounded daily, yearly, or semi-annually and prepayment penalties may apply. There may be legal restrictions on certain matters, and consumer protection laws may specify or prohibit certain practices.

Depending on the size of the loan and the prevailing practice in the country the term may be short (10 years) or long (50 years plus). 25 to 30 years is the usual maximum term though shorter periods, such as 15-year mortgage loans, are common. Mortgage payments, which are typically made monthly, contain a repayment of the principal and an interest. The amount going toward the principal in each payment varies throughout the term of the mortgage. In the early years the repayments are mostly interest. Towards the end of the mortgage, payments are mostly for principal. In this way the payment amount determined at outset is calculated to ensure the loan is repaid at a specified date in the future.

*Interest Only*

The main alternative to a principal and interest mortgage is an interest-only mortgage, where the principal is not repaid throughout the term. This type of mortgage is common especially when associated with a regular investment plan. With this arrangement regular contributions are made to a separate investment plan designed to build up a lump sum to repay the mortgage at maturity. This type of arrangement is called an *investment-backed mortgage* or is often related to the type of plan used: endowment mortgage if an endowment policy is used, similarly a Personal Equity Plan mortgage, Individual Savings Account mortgage or pension mortgage. Investment-backed mortgages are seen as higher risk as are dependent on the investment making sufficient return to clear the debt.

## Interest-only Lifetime Mortgage

*Reverse Mortgage*

- A reverse mortgage (or lifetime mortgage) is a loan available to senior citizens. Reverse mortgage, as its name suggests, is exactly opposite of a typical mortgage, such as a home loan.
- "A reverse mortgage is a loan available to seniors and is used to release the home equity in the property as one lump sum or multiple payments. The homeowner's obligation to repay the loan is deferred until the owner dies, the home is sold, or the owner leaves (e.g., into aged care)" The analysis of definition provides some basic features of reverse mortgage products.

These are:

- The loan is available only to senior citizens owning a home.
- The loan can be in the form of Lump-sum or multiple payments like annuity etc.
- Homeowner does not have obligation to repay the loan till the house is his prime residence The payback is done once the owner dies or leaves the house. This is done though selling the house and recovering the loan through its proceeds. Thus a home owner going for reverse mortgage may take his payment in the following form.
- A lump sum at the beginning (can be used for home improvement health expenses etc)
- Monthly payments till a fixed term
- Monthly payments as a life-long annuity.
- A combination of the above
- Some lenders have come out with plans different from the above to suit the requirements of the borrowers.

## Types of Reverse Mortgage Products

- **Home Reversion or Sale and Lease Back:** The homeowner sells the house but keeps the right to live in the house till the time it is his prime residence. The amount could be used for home improvement, any other health need etc.
- **Interest-only Mortgage:** The borrower takes lump sum and pays only interest during his lifetime. The principal is recovered through the sale of the home
- **Mortgage Annuity/ Home Income**: The loan is used to purchase an annuity for the homeowner. The advantage is that even if the homeowner moves out of the home, the annuity will continue till his death
- **Shared Appreciation Mortgage:** This provides loans at a below market interest rate.. In return, the lender gets a pre-agreed share in any appreciation in the property value over the accumulated value of the loan.

## Pricing of Reverse Mortgage Products

The various considerations which needs to be taken while pricing a product of this nature are

- **Age of the borrower**: If it is a joint borrowing then the age of the younger borrower is considered.
- **Value of the property:** Then value of the property plays a major role in determining the price for an RM product
- **Expected Interest Rate:** As the product resembles the normal annuity product in some sense, the current and expected interest also plays a major role in pricing the product.

## Significance of Reverse Mortgage System in India

The society in India has under-gone huge changes in last 4-5 decades. Nuclear family has replaced the joint family system. The system of family supporting the older people has gone. As mentioned earlier the public pension system has not been able to provide an alternate support to old people. This condition leaves the older people in jeopardy.

The older people face following issues

- Outliving their retirement income
- Depending on their children to help pay expenses.
- Getting sick and having no way to pay the expenses
- Not being able to guarantee an income for their spouse after gone
- Being able to live as long as like in their own home Looking at the current situation, the needs for a product which can help these people to solve some of these problems is always a welcome step.

Reverse mortgage or equity release products tries to answer all these problems. Every Indian, irrespective of its income level tries to build a home for himself during his working life. Reverse mortgage will give him/her an opportunity to generate income from that very home. As the ownership remains with the borrower, can transfer the home to his successors also if the later agrees to pay the loan amount. Such a product relieves the pressure on government also to provide old age security and thus government also needs to support such initiative.

## Risk Inherent in the Reverse Mortgage Product

Any financial product involves some risk and reverse mortgage is no exception. The lender faces many type of risk for this product. Some of these risks are

### i.  *Longevity Risk*

The lender has to provide the payment upfront either lump sum or installments as the case may be but gets his money back only when the borrowers dies or move into another residence. As it is aware that the life expectancy of people is increasing, the risk of late recovery of loans is a big risk for the lenders.

The risk is aggravated by the fact that with the payments from reverse mortgage, the lifestyle of the borrower gets better which may become one of the contributors in the improvement of longevity.

The longevity risk is higher for reverse mortgage where the payment is continued till the death of the borrower since not only the recovery gets delayed but also the lender has to make payments for a longer time.

*ii.    Interest Rate Risk*

The payments to the borrower in case of a reverse mortgage is fixed, either for a term or lifetime but the cash flows for the lender may not be fixed and are dependent on the interest rate market. Thus the lender runs the risk that the interest rates in the market may move in the opposite direction of that the lender anticipated.

*iii.    Market Risk*

The lender in a reverse mortgage can claim back his loan only from the property on which the loan has been granted. He does not have recourse to any other asset of the borrower. If the sales proceeds of the home are not sufficient, the lender cannot clam the balance from the heirs of the borrower. This gives rise to the risk of adverse.

*iv.    Early Redemption Risk*

Some of the reverse mortgages loans may give the borrower an option of repay the loan at any point of time. This leads to another risk for the lender of early redemption as the borrower will pay back the loan when it is most beneficial to him which in most cases does not coincide with the interests of the lender. In case the lender has securitized the loan, which in most of the cases it is, the risk becomes higher as the lender cannot closer its position in this case.

## Risk Mitigation

Risk mitigation is the key for the success of any financial product including reverse mortgage. Some of the risk mitigation techniques which the providers can apply to reduce the risk on their books

i.    **Proper Eligibility Criterions**: The first mitigation of risk can be done at the time of providing loans. This can be done through proper verification of the title of the property, age of the borrower; credit analysis etc. This reduces the risk of default by the borrower

ii.    **Variable Interest Rates Loan as Compared to Fixed Interest Rate Loan:** To avoid interest rate risk, the lender can go for variable interest rates based on some market benchmark like MIBOR. This will also reduce the risk of Pre-payment as the borrower will not have interest arbitrage on prepayment of the loan

iii.    **Proper Analysis of Mortality Trends:** As the product has significant longevity risk, the lender can do a detailed mortality trend analysis on a macro level and also in the market where it is operating.

iv.    **Geographical Diversification:** the lender can look at spreading the business across the country by promoting the product in secondary and tertiary cities also so that the law of large numbers may work properly and if the provider has a bad experience in one market, it can be compensated with good experience in other cities.

## Mortgage Originator

Mortgage Originator is an institution or individual that works with a borrower to complete a mortgage transaction. A mortgage originator can be either a mortgage broker or a mortgage banker, and is the original mortgage lender. Mortgage originators are part of the primary mortgage market.

## Third-Party Mortgage Originator-Definition

1.    A person or company involved in the process of marketing mortgages and gathering borrower information for a mortgage application. This information is then transferred or sold to the actual mortgage lender. Mortgage brokers are third-party originators.

2.    A person or company that is involved in any aspect of the mortgage origination process (underwriting, closing, funding, etc.) on behalf of the actual mortgage lender.

## Loan Originators

The creator of a loan is usually a bank or mortgage broker. A bank might be in the business of creating different types of loans, but the term "origination" typically refers to mortgage loans. The actual person who carries out the loan origination process works for a bank or a mortgage broker and is also called a loan officer or salesperson. Loan originators must pass state and federal testing to become licensed.

## Origination Process

The process of loan origination involves the loan originator examining the potential borrower's application to evaluate the size and type of mortgage the lender is willing to make and guiding the borrower through the paperwork. The loan originator makes a commission, called the loan origination fee, from closing the loan, which is often based on the amount of the mortgage.

## Mortgage Markets

Banks or mortgage brokers often sell the mortgages and originate to other banks, brokers and institutions. The transactions that involve creating a loan form the primary mortgage market, while institutions trading mortgages among themselves constitute the secondary mortgage market. Only the bank or broker that created a mortgage is considered the loan originator. Other institutions may buy the mortgage, but this does not make them the new loan originator.

## Settlement Services

Settlement services includes "any service provided in connection with a real estate settlement including, but not limited to, the following: title searches, title examinations, the provision of title certificates, title insurance, services rendered by an attorney, the preparation of documents, property surveys, the rendering of credit reports or appraisals, pest and fungus inspections, services rendered by a real estate agent or broker, the origination of a federally related mortgage loan, and the handling of the processing, and closing of settlement."

### Settlement Service: Meaning

The term settlement service means "any service provided in connection with a prospective or actual settlement, including, but not limited to, any one or more of the following:

1. Origination of a federally related mortgage loan (including, but not limited to, the taking of loan applications, loan processing, and the underwriting and funding of such loans).
2. Rendering of services by a mortgage broker (including counseling, taking of applications, obtaining verifications and appraisals, and other loan processing and origination services, and communicating with the borrower and lender).
3. Provision of any services related to the origination, processing or funding of a federally related mortgage loan.
4. Provision of title services, including title searches, title examinations, abstract preparation, insurability determinations, and the issuance of title commitments and title insurance policies.
5. Rendering of services by an attorney.
6. Preparation of documents, including notarization, delivery, and recordation.
7. Rendering of credit reports and appraisals.
8. Rendering of inspections, including inspections required by applicable law or any inspections required by the sales contract or mortgage documents prior to transfer of title.
9. Conducting of settlement by a settlement agent and any related services.

10. Provision of services involving mortgage insurance.
11. Provision of services involving hazard, flood, or other casualty insurance or homeowner's warranties.
12. Provision of services involving mortgage life, disability, or similar insurance designed to pay a mortgage loan upon disability or death of a borrower, but only if such insurance is required by the lender as a condition of the loan.
13. Provision of services involving real property taxes or any other assessments or charges on the real property.
14. Rendering of services by a real estate agent or real estate broker; and
15. Provision of any other services for which a settlement service provider requires a borrower or seller to pay."

## Underwriting

Underwriting is the process by which investment bankers raise investment capital from investors on behalf of corporations and governments that are issuing either equity or debt securities. The word "underwriter" originally came from the practice of having each risk-taker write his name under the total amount of risk he was willing to accept at a specified premium. This centuries-old practice continues, in a way, as new issues are usually brought to market by an underwriting syndicate, in which each firm takes the responsibility, as well as the risk, of selling its specific allotment.

### Bank Underwriting

In banking, underwriting is the detailed credit analysis preceding the granting of a loan, based on credit information furnished by the borrower; such underwriting falls into several areas:

a. Consumer loan underwriting includes the verification of such items as employment history, salary and financial statements; publicly available information, such as the borrower's credit history, which is detailed in a credit report; and the lender's evaluation of the borrower's credit needs and ability to pay. Examples include mortgage underwriting.

b. Commercial underwriting consists of the evaluation of financial information provided by small businesses including analysis of the business balance sheet including tangible net worth, the ratio of debt to worth (leverage) and available liquidity. Analysis of the income statement typically includes revenue trends, gross margin, profitability, and debt service coverage.

Underwriting can also refer to the purchase of corporate bonds, commercial paper, government securities, municipal general-obligation bonds by a commercial bank or dealer bank for its own account or for resale to investors. Bank underwriting of corporate securities is carried out through separate holding-company affiliates, called securities affiliates.

## 3 C'S of Underwriting

- Capacity,
- Credit, and
- Collateral

1. **Capacity:**The underwriters will take a close look at debt-to-income ratio. The bank want to see that the borrower have enough money to fulfill the current obligations as well as new mortgage.

2. **Credit:**The credit is perhaps one of the most important factors in the loan approval process. The credit report will reflect how the borrower have handled and managed repaying past bills. It will also predict the ability to make the proposed mortgage payments on time and in full.
3. **Collateral:**An underwriter wants to make sure a loan amount does not exceed a property's value. Otherwise, a lender may not be able to recover a loan's unpaid balance, in the case of a default. This is why an underwriter orders a home appraisal. This report will assess a home's current worth and safeguard a lender from lending too much money.

## Types of Underwriting

### i.    Firm Underwriting

Generally, underwriters agree to buy such number of shares or debentures which are not to be taken up by the public but sometimes, the underwriting agreement provides that the underwriters will purchase certain shares (as greed upon) themselves. Such an agreement of outright purchase of securities with the underwriters is called Firm Underwriting. This liability is in addition to the shares not taken up by the public. Such an agreement creates confidence in the minds of investing public.

### ii.    Sub-Underwriting

In case of large issue, an underwriter does not wish to carry the whole risk on his shoulders, he may enter into the contract with other underwriters to share the risk. This contract entered into between the main underwriter and the other underwrites is called Sub-underwriting and the other underwriters are called Sub-underwriters. The company is nowhere in the picture. Sub-underwriters are offered a commission slightly below the underwriting commission.

### iii.    Syndicate Underwriting

This is an underwriting agreement between the issuing company and 2-3 or more firms of underwriters to underwriters a large issue. The underwriters agree with the company to share the joint responsibility in an agreed ratio. Some-times, these underwriters to the contract form a new consortium or syndicate. Such a system is called Syndicate Underwriting. It is very popular in Germany.

## Importance of Underwriting

### i.    Assurance of Adequate Finance

Underwriting is a guarantee given buy the underwriters to take up the whole issue or remaining shares, not subscribed by public. In the absence an underwriting agreement, a company may face a situation where even minimum subscription is not received and, it will have to go, into liquidation. In case of an existing company, it may have to postpone its projects for which the issue was meant. As a result of an underwriting contract, a company has not to wait till the shares have been subscribed before entering into the required contracts for purchase of fixed assets etc. it can go ahead with its plan confidently. Thus, underwriting agreement assures of the required funds within a reasonable or agreed time.

### ii.    Benefit of Expert Advice

An incidental advantage of underwriting is that the issuing company gets the benefit of expert advice. An underwriter of repute would go into the soundness of the plan put forward by the company before entering into an agreement and suggest changes wherever necessary, enabling the company to avid certain pitfalls.

### iii. *Increase in Goodwill of the Company*

The good underwriters being men or firms of financial integrity an established reputation. As it is already explained that underwriters satisfy themselves with the financial integrity of the company and viability of the plan, the investors therefore, runs much less risk when the investor buy shares or debentures which have been underwritten by them. The underwriters assure of the soundness of the company. Thus, good underwriters increase the goodwill of the company.

### iv. *Geographical Dispersion of Securities*

Generally, underwriters maintain working arrangement with other underwriters and broken throughout the country and in other countries too and as such, are able to tap the financial resources for the company not only in on particular area but also in other areas as well. In this way marketability of securities increases and geographical dispersion of shares and debentures in promoted.

### v. *Service to Prospective Buyers*

Underwriters render useful services to the perspective buyers of securities by giving them expert advice regarding the safe investment in sound companies. Sometimes information published and their expert opinion in respect of various companies. Thus, useful services is rendered to the buyers of securities too.

# 14. INDIAN TRADE MARKET

## Introduction to Indian Trade Market

India is fast emerging as a global leader, what with its vast, natural resources, and huge base of skilled manpower. Combined with cutting edge technology, Indian trade market is making its presence felt all across the world. Indian products and services are seen as of international standards and globally competitive. Trade in India has made good progress on liberalizing trade regimes and cutting tariffs since the recent times, when most of the countries started with reforms. Until quite recently, considerable protection levels reflected in the significant tariff peaks and dispersed protection levels were seen in India. Serious constraints to private activity in infrastructure, economic governance, financial impeded export competitiveness too. Insufficient and unreliable power supply, inhibiting red tape is a few of the many examples of these constraints.

Undertaking considerable industrial deregulation and other structural reforms, trade in India recognizes that strong exports are critical for overall economic growth and poverty reduction. Export-led growth has thus become a key thrust for the trade in India.

Integrating with the global economy, India has recorded strong export growth to the United States and the European Union markets. Getting on intro to Indian trade, it is important to note that Indian government recognizes the need to implement additional reforms and address significant constraints to ensure that Indian trade supports growth and benefits the poor. Continuing with trade reforms has become more complex because of concerns of how these reforms will affect employment, income distribution, poverty and vulnerability. India is focused on WTO negotiations on agricultural trade policies, and there is strong interest in services trade.

Indian trade market has made significant progress in integrating with the rest of the world. But it is interesting to note that intra-regional trade remains very low. The reasons behind these low levels of trade could be attributed to protectionist trade regimes, which discriminated against trade among larger neighbors. The continued conflict between India and Pakistan including transport and trade facilitation constraints has also contributed to these lower intra-regional trades. Seeking to increase cooperation in the areas of harmonization of product standards and customs procedures, travel rules and facilities are a must to ensure an increase in intra-regional trade in goods and services.

## Trading

Trading, on the other hand, is the more frequent buying and selling of financial instruments with the aim of outperforming buy-and-hold investments. There is no ownership of the underlying asset so traders are merely **speculating** on the price movement.

Traders can therefore profit from falling markets as well as rising ones. A trader can buy an asset just like an investor but traders also have the ability to sell an instrument without owning it. This is known as short selling and is why many people are particularly attracted to trading. It is a key concept to understand and is a major reason why traders can outperform buy-and-hold investors.

While investors are often satisfied with annual returns of up to 15% depending on the risk element of the investment, some traders seek to make returns that are a multiple of this, as can benefit from the dips in the market as well as the increases because of the ability to short sell.

The length of time a trader has a position open for can range from seconds to years. This timeframe is entirely up to them and relates to their objectives, account size, risk profile and time commit to trading. Trading requires a more hands on approach than investing and regular assessment of market conditions is essential when traders have open positions. A financial instrument is a tradable asset of any kind i.e. it is an asset which can buy or sell at a monetary value on a financial market. So any movement in price of the physical asset will see a similar move in the price of the contract.

# 15.    Letter of Credit

A **letter of credit** is a document issued by a third party that guarantees payment for goods or services when the seller provides acceptable documentation. Letters of credit are usually issued by banks or other financial institutions, but some creditworthy financial services companies, like insurance companies or mutual funds, might issue letters of credit under certain circumstances.

## Elements of a Letter of Credit

- A payment undertaking given by a bank (issuing bank)
- On behalf of a buyer (applicant)
- To pay a seller (beneficiary) for a given amount of money
- On presentation of specified documents representing the supply of goods
- Within specified time limits
- Documents must conform to terms and conditions set out in the letter of credit
- Documents to be presented at a specified place

## Parties to Letter of Credit

A letter of credit generally has three participants.

- First, there is the **beneficiary**, the person or company who will be paid.
- Next, there is the **buyer** or **applicant** of the goods or services. This is the one who needs the letter of credit.
- Finally, there is the **issuing bank**, the institution issuing the letter of credit.

In addition, the beneficiary may request payment to an **advising bank**, which is a bank where the beneficiary is a client, rather than directly to the beneficiary.

Letters of credit are most often used in international trade, where are governed by the **Uniform Customs and Practice for Documentary Credits (or UCP)**, the rules of the International Chamber of Commerce.

**Beneficiary**: It is important to note that the letter of credit transaction is actually a separate contract from the sales contract between the buyer and the seller. The letter of credit transaction deals in documents and not in the handling of goods, and the bank that issues the letter of credit is not liable for the performance of the sales contract between the buyer and the seller. The bank that issued the letter of credit is obligated to pay the specified amount to the seller/beneficiary if it produces the documentation required by the letter of credit. The issuing bank's obligation to its customer, the buyer, is to examine thoroughly all of the documents to insure that meet all the terms and conditions required by the letter of credit. When the beneficiary presents the documents for payment, the beneficiary guarantees that all of the conditions of the letter of credit have been met. Then if the issuing bank's examination of the documents confirms this fact, then the issuing bank makes the specified payment to the beneficiary/seller.

**Issuing Bank:** Once the issuing bank has received the documents and approved them as complying with all of the requirements specified in the letter of credit, the bank is obligated to make payment to the beneficiary. The Uniform Customs and Practice for Documentary Credits allow the issuing bank a reasonable amount of time after receipt of the documents to examine them and to honor the letter of credit by making the specified payment to the beneficiary. Then the issuing bank completes the transaction by receiving reimbursement from the bank customer for whom the letter of credit was issued.

A letter of credit typically will require at a bare minimum documents such as an official invoice, a bill of lading or airway bill, and an insurance document. However, letters of credit may require additional documentation depending upon the nature of the transaction.

**Advising Bank:** An advising bank is usually a bank located in the beneficiary's city. The advising bank's role is to advise the beneficiary and insure the beneficiary that the letter of credit is valid, usually accomplished by having a relationship with or simply by knowing of and communicating with the issuing bank. Also, it is the responsibility of the advising bank to make sure that the appropriate documents are collected and sent to the issuing bank.

**Confirming Bank:** Irrevocable letters of credit may be confirmed or unconfirmed. An issuing bank that issues a confirmed letter of credit may require that a confirming bank confirm the letter of credit for the beneficiary, which means that the confirming bank obligates itself to insure payment to the beneficiary under the letter of credit. Before a confirming bank confirms a letter of credit, it performs an evaluation of the issuing bank and the documentation requirements of the letter of credit. Typically, the confirming bank is also the advising bank, but this is not a requirement, and the functions may be separated.

## Documentation Requirements

In order to receive payment, the beneficiary must present documentation of completion of their part in the transaction to the issuing bank. The documents that the issuing bank will accept are specified in the letter of credit, but may often include:

- Bills of exchange.
- Invoices.
- Government documents such as licenses, certificates of origin, inspection certificates, embassy legalizations, and phyto sanitary certificates.
- Shipping and transport documents such as bills of lading and airway bills.
- Insurance policies or certificates, except cover notes.

The three key documents described in the following:

- Letter of credit
- Draft and
- Bill of lading

These constitute a system developed and modified over centuries to protect both importer and exporter from the risk of non completion of the trade transaction as well as to provide a means of financing.

The three key trade documents are part of a carefully constructed system to determine who bears the financial loss if one of the parties defaults at any time.

**Letter of Credit:** A letter of credit is a bank's promise to pay issued by a bank at the request of an importer, in which the bank promises to pay an exporter upon presentation of documents specified in the Letter of Credit. A Letter of Credit reduces the risk of non completion, because the bank agrees to pay against documents rather than actual merchandise.

An **importer** (buyer) and **exporter** (seller) agree on a transaction and the importer then applies to its local bank for the issuance of an Letter of Credit.

The importer's bank issues an Letter of Credit and cuts a sales contract based on its assessment of the importer's creditworthiness, or the bank might require a cash deposit or other collateral from the importer in advance. The importer's bank will want to know the type of transaction, the amount of money involved, and what documents must accompany the draft that will be drawn against the Letter of Credit. If the importer's bank is satisfied with the credit standing of the applicant, it will issue an Letter of Credit guaranteeing to pay for the merchandise if shipped in accordance with the instructions and conditions contained in the

Letter of Credit. The essence of an Letter of Credit is the promise of the issuing bank to pay against specified documents, which must accompany any draft drawn against the credit. The Letter of Credit is not a guarantee of the underlying commercial transaction. Indeed, the Letter of Credit is a separate transaction from any sales or other contracts on which it might be based.

To constitute a true Letter of Credit transaction, the following elements must be present with respect to the issuing bank:

1. The issuing bank must receive a fee or other valid business consideration for issuing the Letter of Credit.
2. The bank's Letter of Credit must contain a specified expiration date or a definite maturity.
3. The bank's commitment must have a stated maximum amount of money.
4. The bank's obligation to pay must arise only on the presentation of specific documents, and the bank must not be called on to determine disputed questions of fact or law.
5. The bank's customer must have an unqualified obligation to reimburse the bank on the same condition as the bank has paid.

This is a sample of documents that may be required in a letter of credit transaction:

- Financial Documents: For example, a bill of exchange or a Co-accepted Draft.
- Commercial Documents: For example, Invoice, Packing List.
- Shipping Documents: For example, Transport Document, Insurance Certificate, Commercial, Official or Legal Documents.
- Official Documents: For example, License, Embassy Legalization, Certificate of Origin, Inspection Certificate, Phyto-sanitary Certificate, Agricultural Certifications.
- Transport Documents: For example, Bill of Lading, Order Bill of Lading, Through Bill of Lading, Airway Bill, Trucking Receipt, Railway Receipt, Mate Receipt, Forwarder Cargo Receipt, Rail Consignment Note, Road Consignment Note, Consignment Instructions, Delivery Receipt.
- Insurance documents: For example, Insurance Policy, or Insurance Certificate.

## Characteristics of Letter of Credit

### Negotiability

Letters of credit are usually negotiable. The issuing bank is obligated to pay not only the beneficiary, but also any bank nominated by the beneficiary. Negotiable instruments are passed freely from one party to another almost in the same way as money. To be negotiable, the letter of credit must include an unconditional promise to pay, on demand or at a definite time. The nominated bank becomes a holder in due course. As a holder in due course, the holder takes the letter of credit for value, in good faith, without notice of any claims against it. A holder in due course is treated favorably under the UCC.

The transaction is considered a straight negotiation if the issuing bank's payment obligation extends only to the beneficiary of the credit. If a letter of credit is a straight negotiation it is referenced on its face by "we engage with you" or "available with ourselves". Under these conditions the promise does not pass to a purchaser of the draft as a holder in due course.

### Revocability

Letters of credit may be either revocable or irrevocable. A revocable letter of credit may be revoked or modified for any reason, at any time by the issuing bank without notification. A revocable letter of credit cannot be confirmed. If a correspondent bank is engaged in a transaction that involves a revocable letter of credit, it serves as the advising bank.

Once the documents have been presented and meet the terms and conditions in the letter of credit, and the draft is honored, the letter of credit cannot be revoked. The revocable letter of credit is not a commonly used instrument. It is generally used to provide guidelines for shipment. If a letter of credit is revocable it would be referenced on its face.

The irrevocable letter of credit may not be revoked or amended without the agreement of the issuing bank, the confirming bank, and the beneficiary. An irrevocable letter of credit from the issuing bank insures the beneficiary that if the required documents are presented and the terms and conditions are complied with, payment will be made. If a letter of credit is irrevocable it is referenced on its face.

*Transfer and Assignment*

The beneficiary has the right to transfer or assign the right to draw, under a credit only when the credit states that it is transferable or assignable. Credits governed by the Uniform Commercial Code (Domestic) maybe transferred an unlimited number of times. Under the Uniform Customs Practice for Documentary Credits (International) the credit may be transferred only once. However, even if the credit specifies that it is nontransferable or non assignable, the beneficiary may transfer their rights prior to performance of conditions of the credit.

*Sight and Time Drafts*

All letters of credit require the beneficiary to present a draft and specified documents in order to receive payment. A draft is a written order by which the party creating it, orders another party to pay money to a third party. A draft is also called a bill of exchange.

## Types and Features of Letters of Credit

Most letters of credit are **import/export letters of credit**, which, as the name implies, are letters of credit that are used in international trade. The same letter of credit would be termed an import letter of credit by the importer and an export letter of credit by the exporter. In most cases, the importer is the buyer and the exporter is the beneficiary.

Commercial letters of credit are also classified as follows:

**Irrevocable versus Revocable**: The irrevocable letter of credit only allows change or cancellation of the letter of credit by the issuing bank after application by the buyer and approval by the beneficiary. All letters of credit governed by the current UCP are irrevocable letters of credit. An irrevocable L/C obligates the issuing bank to honor drafts drawn in compliance with the credit and can be neither canceled nor modified without the consent of all parties, including in particular the beneficiary (exporter).

A revocable L/C can be canceled or amended at any time before payment; it is intended to serve as a means of arranging payment but not as a guarantee of payment. The **revocable letter of credit** can be changed at any time by either the buyer or the issuing bank with no notification to the beneficiary. The most recent version of the UCP, UCP 600, did away with this form of letter of credit for any transaction under their jurisdiction.

**Confirmed versus Unconfirmed**: A **confirmed letter of credit** is one where a second bank agrees to pay the letter of credit at the request of the issuing bank. While not usually required by law, an issuing bank might be required by court order to only issue confirmed letters of credit if in receivership. An L/C issued by one bank can be confirmed by another bank. In case the confirming bank undertakes to honor drafts drawn in compliance with the credit.

An **unconfirmed L/C** is the obligation only of the issuing bank. An exporter is likely to want a foreign bank's L/C confirmed by a domestic bank when the exporter has doubts about the foreign bank's ability to pay. Such doubts can arise when the exporter is unsure of the financial standing of the foreign bank, or if political or economic conditions in the foreign country are unstable. An unconfirmed letter of credit is guaranteed only by the issuing bank. This is the most common form with regard to confirmation.

**Documentary Credit:** Required some specific documents.

**Clean LC:** Shipping documents are not required. It is used for paymentv of service rendered by any consultant or any person & firm etc. Drafts and beneficiary's invoice are required for negotiation purpose.

**Confirmed LC:** LC which is confirmed by Bank in addition to issuing Bank.

**Revolving LC:** Original amount will automatically revive after shipment & negotiation thus original amount will come into existence.

**Transferable Credit:** The opening bankv is authorized advising Bank to transfer the credit to any other party or beneficiary in lieu of existing beneficiary. A letter of credit may also be a **transferrable letter of credit**. These are commonly used when the beneficiary is simply an intermediary for the real supplier of the goods and services or is one of a group of suppliers. It allows the named beneficiary to present its own documentation but transfer all or part of the payment to the actual suppliers.

An **un-transferrable letter of credit** does not allow transfer of payments to third parties. A letter of credit may also be **at sight**, which is payable as soon as the documentation has been presented and verified, or payment may be **deferred**. Deferred letters of credit are also called a **Usance letter of credit** and may be put off until a certain time period has passed or the buyer has had the opportunity to inspect or even sell the related goods.

A **red clause** letter of credit allows the beneficiary to receive partial payment before shipping the products or performing the services. Originally, these terms were written in red ink, hence the name. In practical use, issuing banks will rarely offer these terms unless the beneficiary is very creditworthy or an advising bank agrees to refund the money if the shipment is not made.

Finally, a **back-to-back letter of credit** is used in a trade involving an intermediary, such as a trading house. It is actually made up of two letters of credit, one issued by the buyer's bank to the intermediary and the other issued by the intermediary's bank to the seller.

## Benefits of a Letter of Credit

*To The Exporter/Seller*

- Letters of credit open doors to international trade by providing a secure mechanism for payment upon fulfillment of contractual obligations.
- A bank is substituted for the buyer as the source of payment for goods or services exported.
- The issuing bank undertakes to make payment, provided all the terms and conditions stipulated in the letter of credit are complied with.
- Financing opportunities, such as pre-shipment finance secured by a letter of credit and/or discounting of accepted drafts drawn under letters of credit, are available in many countries.
- Bank expertise is made available to help complete trade transactions successfully.
- Payment for the goods shipped can be remitted to own bank or a bank at choice.

- Payment will only be made to the seller when the terms and conditions of the letter of credit are complied with.
- The importer can control the shipping dates for the goods being purchased.
- Cash resources are not tied up.

## Risks in Letter of Credit Transactions

Letter of credit transactions are not without risks. The risks inherent in these types of transactions include:

- **Fraud risk**, in which the payment is obtained through the use of falsified or forged documents for worthless or nonexistent merchandise
- **Regulatory risk**, in which government action may prevent completion of the transaction
- **Legal risk**, in which legal action prevents completion of the transaction
- **Force majeure risk**, in which completion of the transaction is prevented by an external force, such as war or natural disaster
- **Failure of the issuing or collecting bank**

A **collection agency**, also known as a debt collector, is a business or other entity that specializes in debt **collection**, i.e. pursues payments of debts owed by individuals or businesses. Most **collection agencies** operate as agents of creditors and **collect** debts for a fee or percentage of the total amount owed.

## Documentary Collections

Collections terms offer an important bank payment mechanism that can serve the needs of both the exporter and importer. Under this arrangement, the sale transaction is settled by the bank through an exchange of documents, thus enabling simultaneous payment and transfer of title. The importer is not obliged to pay for goods prior to shipment and the exporter retains title to the goods until the importer either pays for the value of the draft upon presentation (sight draft) or accept to pay at a later date and time (term draft). The principal obligations of parties to a documentary collection arrangement are set out in the guidelines of the "Uniform Rules for Collection" (URC) drafted by the Paris-based International Chamber of Commerce.

### Role of Banks in Documentary Collections

Banks play essential roles in transactions utilizing documentary collections as follows:

**Remitting Bank:** This is the exporter's bank and acts as the exporter's agent in collecting payment from the importer. It basically transmits the exporter's instructions along with the terms of the draft to the importer's bank. The bank does not assume any risks and does not undertake to pay the exporter but can influence to obtain settlement of a bill.

**Collecting Bank:** This is the importer's bank and takes up the role of ensuring that the buyer pays (or accept to pay) for the goods before shipping documents are released to him.

Generally, the banks in the transaction control the flow and transfer of documents and regulate the timing of the transaction. The safety of the documents is must in their possession but are not responsible for their validity and accuracy.

*Variations of Documentary Collections*

This form of trade settlement comes in two forms-Documents against Payment and Documents against Acceptance. Each of these forms of collections may be either "clean" (financial document alone) or "documentary" (commercial documents with or without a financial document). A financial document is a check or a draft; a commercial document is a bill of lading or other shipping document. A clean collection involves dollar-denominated drafts and checks presented for collection to U.S. banks by their foreign correspondents. In a documentary collection, the exporter draws a draft or bill of exchange directly on the importer and presents this draft, with shipping documents attached, to the bank for collection.

**Cash against documents/Sight Drafts:** In a transaction on documents against payment, the exporter releases the shipping documents to the importer only on payment for the goods. In this arrangement, the exporter retains title to goods on board and may decide to refuse their discharge if payments are not received. This arrangement which demands the buyer's immediate payment of the exporter relies on a sight draft drawn on the buyer.

**Document against Acceptance/Term Drafts:** An exporter may decide to release shipping documents to a buyer on acceptance of the exporter's drafts. In this case, the importer is under an obligation to pay at a future date. This method satisfies both parties since the importer is able to receive the goods before payment and the exporter has a firm assurance (but no guarantee) that payment will come at a specified future date.

*Flow of Transaction in a Documentary Collections Deal*

1. Exporter/drawer and Importer/drawee agree on a sales contract, including payment to be made under a Documentary Collection.
2. The Exporter ships the merchandise to the foreign buyer and receives in exchange the shipping documents.
3. Immediately thereafter, the Exporter presents the shipping documents with detailed instructions for obtaining payment to his bank (Remitting bank).
4. The Remitting bank sends the documents along with the Exporter's instructions to a designated bank in the importing country (Collecting Bank).
5. Depending on the terms of the sales contract, the Collecting Bank would release the documents to the importer only upon receipt of payment or acceptance of draft from the buyer. (The importer will then present the shipping documents to the carrier in exchange for the goods).
6. Having received payment, the collecting bank forwards proceeds to the Remitting Bank for the exporter's account.
7. Once payment is received, the Remitting bank credits the Exporter's account, less its charges.

## Advantages and Disadvantages of Documentary Collection

The major advantage of a "cash against documents" payment method for the Buyer is the low cost, versus opening a Letter of Credit. The advantage for the Seller is that he can receive full payment prior to releasing control of the documents, although this is offset by the risk that the Buyer will, for some reason, reject the documents. Since the cargo would already be loaded, the Seller has little recourse against the Buyer in cases of non-payment. A payment against documents arrangement involves a high level of trust between the Seller and the Buyer and should be adopted only by parties well known to each other.

## Risks in Documentary Collections

**For the Exporter:** If it is a sight draft, the exporter will reduce the risk of non-payment but will not eliminate it totally since the importer may not be in a position to pay for the goods or may not be able to procure sufficient foreign exchange to make the payment. In this case the exporter may be forced to either call back the goods or negotiate sale to some other interested party, which may be at a reduced rate.

In the case of term draft, the risk to the exporter is higher since the foreign buyer will take possession of the goods and may not pay at due date, forcing therefore the exporter to try and collect payment from the foreign buyer in the foreign buyer's home country.

**For the Importer:** The importer faces the risk of paying for goods of sub-standard quality or even with shortages. In such a circumstance, it would take some time to get refunds from the exporter. It could also happen that the exporter refuses to make refunds, leading the importer to lengthy legal proceedings.

# 16.   BANK GUARANTEE

This is a surety that is provided by a bank or a financial institution that will pay off the debts and liabilities incurred by an individual or a business entity in case unable to do so. This enables a business to grow and expand by deferring payment of goods and services. This helps a business to invest on a larger scale than would have been possible without the bank guarantee.

By providing a guarantee, a bank offers to honor any payment to the creditors upon receiving a request. This requires that the financial institution be very sure of the business or individual to whom the bank guarantee is being issued. So, banks run risk assessments to ensure that the guaranteed sum can be retrieved back from the business. This may require the business to furnish a security in the shape of cash or capital assets. Any entity that can pass the risk assessment and provide security may obtain a bank guarantee.

## Operation of Bank Guarantees

The system for providing bank guarantees work like this:

- Applicant and the creditor ascertain that there is a need for a bank guarantee.
- Applicant reaches out to a financial institution to issue a bank guarantee to the creditor.
- The bank runs a risk assessment and asks for a security.
- The applicant furnishes the security and the bank, or the financial institution processes the bank guarantee.
- The bank guarantee is sent to the creditor's bank or the creditor, or the applicant may be asked to collect it in person to give it to their creditor.

## Advantages of Bank Guarantee

A business benefits from a bank guarantee as:

- It allows one to defer payment for goods or services procured on the basis of the security provided by the bank guarantee.
- All the money is not tied up in one project but can be spread around.
- There is the cash available to explore and expand business.

## Types of Bank Guarantee

There are in general two types of Bank Guarantee:

1. Direct bank guarantee is a guarantee which is issued by the bank of the account holder directly in favour of the Beneficiary.
2. Indirect guarantee is a guarantee which is issued by a second bank in return for a counter-guarantee.

A financial institution can provide many different types of bank guarantees. These include the following:

- **Performance Guarantee** (or Performance Bond): These are bonds that act as collateral for any loss suffered by the buyer in case the performance of the seller is below par.
- **Advance Payment Guarantee**: This is to ensure the safety of any advance payment made by the buyers to the seller. In case the seller is unable to deliver the service or the goods, then the buyer can get his money back.
- **Payment Guarantee**: This guarantee is provided to the seller, ensuring payment by a predetermined date.

- **Conditional Payment Undertaking**: This is an instruction to the bank from an account holder to pay a sum of money to a creditor on completion of certain conditions. This bond is a post contract instrument that is used to pay off agents and contractor on completion of a project.
- **Guarantee Securing Credit Line**: This surety is given to a creditor on claims against the debtor in case a loan is not repaid as per the terms of the agreement.
- **Order and Counter Guarantee**: This is a surety given by the debtor to the creditor, to protect against the failure to fulfill an obligation as contracted. In case of default, the creditor can demand the payment back.

# 17.  LOAN

## Introduction

A **loan** is to receive money from a friend, bank or financial institution in exchange for future repayment of the **principal**, plus **interest**. The principal is the amount borrowed, and the interest is the amount charged for receiving the loan. Since lenders are taking a risk that may not repay the loan, they have to offset that risk by charging a fee-known as interest. Loans typically are **secured** or **unsecured**. A secured loan involves pledging an asset (such as a car, boat or house) as collateral for the loan. If the borrower **defaults**, or doesn't pay back the loan, the lender takes possession of the asset. An unsecured loan option is preferred, but not as common. If the borrower doesn't pay back the unsecured loan, the lender doesn't have the right to take anything in return.

## Types of Loans

**Personal Loans**: These loans received at almost any bank. Personal loans are often unsecured and fairly easy to get if there is average credit history. The downside is that are usually for small amounts and the interest rates are higher than secured loans.

**Cash Advances**: Cash advances from the credit card company or other payday loan institutions are an option. These loans are easy to get, but can have extremely high interest rates. These loans should really only be considered when there are no other alternative ways to get money.

**Student Loans**: These are great ways to help finance a college education. The most common loans are Stafford loans and Perkins loans. The interest rates are very reasonable, and usually don't have to pay the loans back.

**Mortgage Loans**: This is most likely the biggest loan. These loans are secured by the house or property. That means if not made the payments in a timely manner, the bank or lender can take the house or property back.  Mortgages help people get into homes that would otherwise take years to save for. The loans are often structured in 10, 15 or 30-year terms, and the interest to pay is tax-deductible and fairly low compared to other loans.

**Home-equity Loans and Lines of Credit:** Homeowners can borrow against equity on their house with these types of loans. The equity or loan amount would be the difference between the appraised value of home and the amount still owe on mortgage. These loans are good for home additions, home improvements or debt consolidation. The interest rate is often tax deductible and also fairly low compared to other loans.

**Small Business Loans**: The local banks usually offer these loans to people looking to start a business. The borrower do require a little more work than normal and often require a business plan to show the validity of what doing. These are often secured loans, so will have to pledge some personal assets as collateral in case the business fails.

www.ingramcontent.com/pod-product-compliance
Lightning Source LLC
LaVergne TN
LVHW041327200726
843509LV00009B/639